To the Reader:

Scientology® religious philosophy contains pastoral counseling procedures intended to assist an individual to gain greater knowledge of self.
The mission of the Church of Scientology is a simple one: to help the
individual achieve greater self-confidence and personal integrity, thereby
enabling him to really trust and respect himself and his fellow man. The
attainment of the benefits and goals of Scientology philosophy requires each individual's dedicated participation, as only through his own efforts can he achieve
these.

This book is part of the religious literature and works of the Scientology
Founder, L. Ron Hubbard. It is presented to the reader as part of the record of his
personal research into life, and the application of same by others, and should be
construed only as a written report of such research and not as a statement of claims
made by the Church or the Founder.

Scientology philosophy and its forerunner, Dianetics® spiritual healing technology, as practiced by the Church, address only the "thetan" (spirit). Although
the Church, as are all churches, is free to engage in spiritual healing, it does not, as
its primary goal is increased spiritual awareness for all. For this reason, the
Church does not wish to accept individuals who desire treatment of physical or
mental illness but prefers to refer these to qualified specialists of other organizations
who deal in these matters.

The Hubbard® Electrometer is a religious artifact in the Church Confessional.
It in itself does nothing, and is used by ministers only to assist parishioners in
locating areas of spiritual distress or travail.

We hope the reading of this book is only the first stage of a personal
voyage of discovery into this new and vital world religion.

This Book Belongs to:

_____

_____
(Date)

Church of Scientology International

THE
PROBLEMS
OF WORK

L. RON HUBBARD

THE PROBLEMS OF WORK

PUBLICATIONS, INC.

A HUBBARD PUBLICATION

Published in the U.S.A. by
Bridge Publications, Inc.
4751 Fountain Avenue
Los Angeles, California 90029

ISBN 0-88404-377-0

Published in other countries by
NEW ERA® Publications International ApS
Store Kongensgade 55
1264 Copenhagen K, Denmark

ISBN 87-7336-575-0

Important Note

In reading this book, be very certain you never go past a word you do not fully understand.

The only reason a person gives up a study or becomes confused or unable to learn is because he or she has gone past a word that was not understood.

The confusion or inability to grasp or learn comes AFTER a word that the person did not have defined and understood.

Have you ever had the experience of coming to the end of a page and realizing you didn't know what you had read? Well, somewhere earlier on that page you went past a word that you had no definition for or an incorrect definition for.

Here's an example. "It was found that when the crepuscule arrived the children were quieter and when it was not present, they were much livelier." You see what happens. You think you don't understand the whole idea, but the inability to understand came entirely from the one word you could not define, *crepuscule*, which means twilight or darkness.

It may not only be the new and unusual words that you will

have to look up. Some commonly used words can often be misdefined and so cause confusion.

This datum about not going past an undefined word is the most important fact in the whole subject of study. Every subject you have taken up and abandoned had its words which you failed to get defined.

Therefore, in studying this book be very, very certain you never go past a word you do not fully understand. If the material becomes confusing or you can't seem to grasp it, there will be a word just earlier that you have not understood. Don't go any further, but go back to BEFORE you got into trouble, find the misunderstood word and get it defined.

Definitions

As an aid to the reader, words most likely to be misunderstood have been defined in footnotes the first time they occur in the text. Words sometimes have several meanings. The footnote definitions in this book only give the meaning that the word has as it is used in the text. Other definitions for the word can be found in a dictionary.

A glossary including all the footnote definitions is at the back of this book.

Contents

Introduction

Scientology, the broad science of life, has many applications.

If you knew what life was doing, you would know what many sciences and activities were doing.

Here, we have Scientology assisting the worker and the executive in helping man to be more competent and more able, less tired and more secure in the workaday world.

Scientology is already being applied in many of the larger businesses of Earth. They have found they could use it.

L. Ron Hubbard

1

On What Does Holding a Job Depend?

1

On What Does Holding a Job Depend?

On what does holding a job depend?

Familial connections? Who you know? Personal charm? Luck? Education? Industry?[1] Interest? Intelligence? Personal ability?

To one grown old and even somewhat cynical[2] in the world of work, the first several seem to have dominance. Only the young appear to be left with the illusion or delusion that personal ability, intelligence, interest, education and industry have anything to do with it; and the very, very cynical would have us believe that indeed these are only the symptoms of being very young.

We have too often seen the son become the foreman, the new son-in-law, yesterday the shipping clerk, soar to board membership; and we all too often have known that the son and son-in-law not only had no aptitude in the first place but that

---

1. **industry:** getting things done actively and purposefully; application of energy or purpose to work.

2. **cynical:** believing that people are motivated in all their actions only by selfishness; denying the sincerity of people's motives and actions or the value of living.

with no fear of discipline they act more carelessly of the firm than the worst employee present. Familial connection is something dependent upon the accident of birth.

But, leaving familial connection until some other day, what have we left? There is who you know. Personal connection plays a dominant part in obtaining, keeping and improving a position, there can be no doubt of this. One has a friend who works for the Jim-Jambo Company; the friend knows of an opening; the friend has other friends and these still other friends and so into the Jim-Jambo Company one can settle down and work with some security and hope of rise.

And then there is the matter of personal charm. How often have we seen the young stenographer who couldn't spell *cat* suddenly soar, with her typing fingers still all thumbs, to the post of the executive secretary to the boss, wherein, while she can't spell *cat* any better, she can certainly spell *raise* and raise again and perhaps even *supper club* or *diamond necklace*. And we have also seen the young man with a good "front"[3] soar above his elders because he could perhaps tell the right joke or play a slightly worse game of golf.

We have seen, too, the factor of education all gone awry in firms and governments and the trained man, at how much cost of eyesight become learned beyond credit, yet passed over for some chap who didn't have a degree to his name beyond a certain degree of push. We have seen the untutored madly ordering the millions and the wise advising a score.

Industry as well seems to have scant[4] place to those cynical

---

3. **front:** an appearance, usually pretended or assumed, of social standing, wealth, etc.

4. **scant:** inadequate in size or amount; not enough; meager.

---

few of us who have seen it all. The eagerness of the young to slave is all too often braked by the older head who says, "Why get in a sweat about it, young'un?[5] It'll all come out the same." And perhaps we've stayed after hours and daubed ourselves with ink, or lingered at our post beyond all demand of duty, only to watch in times to come the lazy one we scorned draw the better pay. And we've said it isn't justice—something less than that.

And interest, too, we've seen come all to naught. When our absorption in the deadly game of firm or unit with its rivals made us lay aside neglected our own wife, or life, and when we've burned the night and leisure time to work out solutions gauged to save our firm, and have sent them in, and have had them come back, neglected, and soon have beheld our fellow worker, whose total interest was a man or stamps and not the firm at all, go up to higher posts, we had some cause to be less interested, we thought. And interest in our work became condemned by those around us who, not understanding it, became tired of hearing it in our mouths.

Intelligence, against this hard-beaten parade of broken illusions, would seem to have no bearing whatever upon our fates. When we see the stupid rule the many, when we see the plans and decisions passed which would have been condemned even by the children of the workers, we wonder what intelligence could have to do with it. Better to be dumb, we might come to think, than have our own wits continually outraged by the stupidities which pass for company planning.

Personal ability, against this torrent, this confusing chaos of random causes for promotion and better pay, would seem a wasted item. We have seen our own wasted. We have seen the

---

5. **young'un:** slang for "young one" or child.

abilities of others scorned. We have seen the unable rise while the able remained neglected or even unemployed. So personal ability would not seem the factor it might once have been to us, small cogwheels in the clashing gears of business fate. It must then certainly be luck and nothing but luck the whole way down.

And so it seems to appear even to an "experienced" eye that the obtaining, the holding, and the improving of a job are all dependent upon a chaos of causes, all of them out of our control. We accept, instead of orderly expectancy, a tumbling mass of accidentals as our fate.

We try a little. We dress well and cleanly in order to apply for a position; we take ourselves to the place of work daily; we shuffle the papers or the boxes or the machinery parts in a fashion we hope will pass; we leave by crowded transport to our homes and expect another day's dull toil.

Occasionally we start up a correspondence course to give us a small edge on our fellows—and often drop it before it is done: it seems that we cannot even do this little to help us on our way against this flood of accidentals.

We become ill. We run out of sick leave. Still but hardly recovered we now have no job. We become the victims of an accidental cabal[6] or slander[7] and we have no job. We are thrust up against jobs we cannot do and then again we have no job. We grow too old, our time is spent in remembering how fast we once were, and one day we have no job.

---

6. **cabal:** a secret plot.

7. **slander:** the utterance in the presence of another person of a false statement or statements, damaging to a third person's character or reputation.

The lot[8] of the man in the workaday world is uncertainty. His goal is security. But only few attain this goal. The rest of us worry from day to day, from year to year, about our ability to get work, hold work, improve our lots. And all too often our worst fears take place. Once we had the rich to look toward and envy, but now the taxes which we bear have reduced, despite their clever accountants, even their number. States and governments rise and promise us all security and then give us restrictions which make that seem shaky, too.

From day to day new threats impose themselves on our consciousness. A world where the machine is king makes man a cog, and we are told of new developments which do the work of thousands of us and so we starve.

The advertisements thrust at us, in our transports, newspapers, streets, radios and TV, all manner of things to own. And no matter how delightful they are to own, *we* the men who make them can't own them—not on our pay. And Christmases leave us a little ashamed at how little we can buy and we make the coat do just another year. And the years advance and we grow no younger. And each hour confronts us with the accidents which might make or break our futures. No wonder we believe in luck alone.

Well, there is the problem.

To eat we must have a job. To live we must continue to be acceptable on our jobs. To better ourselves we must hope for the breaks.[9] And it all appears a huge, disheartening confusion composed of accidents, good luck and bad luck, or drudgery with nothing to win at the end of it.

---

8. **lot:** one's position in life; fortune.

9. **breaks:** chance pieces of luck, often specifically of good luck.

What would you give for something to lift you out of such ruts? Perhaps you are not in them, but if not you're one of the lucky ones. Men, to escape these ruts, have perpetrated[10] the bloodiest wars and revolutions of history. Whole dynasties[11] have been cut to the dust in an overpowering convulsion[12] born from despair. Jobs get few. Holding them becomes more and more accidental. At last none can longer stand the strain of insecurity and the answer is raw, red revolution. And does this come to anything? No. Revolution is that act of displacing a tyranny with a tyranny ten times more despotic[13] than the old. Changing governments, not even changing firms can change basic security.

The quest for security is a quest for constancy and peace. A worker deserves these things. He creates the goods. He should have the wherewithal[14] to live. Instead, he has a chaos.

But where is this chaos? Is it in the worker's family? Some say so. Is it in the character of capital?[15] Some say so. Is this chaos born of bad government? Many have said so. Is it in the worker himself? Some would like him to think that.

No, it is not in any of these things. The chaos of insecurity exists in the chaos of data about work and about people. If you have no compasses by which to steer through life, you get lost. So many recent elements—of the Industrial Age—have entered into life that life itself needs to be better understood.

---

10. **perpetrated:** done or performed (something evil, criminal or offensive); been guilty of.

11. **dynasties:** successions of rulers who are members of the same family.

12. **convulsion:** any violent disturbance, as a social upheaval or an earthquake.

13. **despotic:** having unrestricted power.

14. **wherewithal:** the things (especially money) needed for a purpose.

15. **capital:** wealth (money or property) owned or used in business by a person, corporation, etc.

Work and security are parts of life. If life is not understood then neither will these parts of life be understood. If all life seems chaotic, a matter of guess and chance, then certainly work will seem chaotic.

But the role of work in existence is a greater role than any other. Some say we spend a third of our lives in bed and therefore beds are important. But we spend more than a third of our lives at work and if we don't work we don't have a bed, so it seems that work is more important by far. If you add up the various parts of life, love or sports or entertainment, you will find that the majority of concentration is not on any of these but upon *work*. Work is the major role of our existences whether we like it or not. If we don't like it, we don't like life.

If we find a man a bit insane, old-time ologies[16] would have had us look up his love life or his childhood. A newer idea and a better one is to look up his security and conditions of work. As security goes bad in a nation, insanity rises. If we were to attack national insanity problems and conquer them we wouldn't build better insane asylums—we would better the conditions of work.

Life is seven-tenths work, one-tenth familial, one-tenth political and one-tenth relaxation. Economics—the paycheck, struggle for—is seven-tenths of existence. Lose a man his income or his job and you find him in bad mental condition, usually. If we're going to find proofs of this anywhere, we'll find them everywhere. Worry over security, worry over worth, worries about being able to do things in life for others, are the principal worries of existence. Let's be very simple. People with nothing to do, people without purpose most easily become neurotic[17] or

---

16. **ologies:** branches of learning; science: a humorous usage.

17. **neurotic:** behavior characterizing one who is insane or disturbed on some subject (as opposed to a psychotic person, who is just insane in general).

mad. Work, basically, is not a drudgery, it is something to do. The paycheck tells us we are worth something. And of course it buys us what we have to have to live. Or almost does.

All right. Work-security, then, is important. But security itself is an understanding. Insecurity is *unknownness*. When one is insecure, he simply doesn't know. He is not sure. Men who *know* are secure. Men who don't know believe in luck. One is made insecure by not knowing whether or not he is going to be sacked. Thus he worries. And so it is with all insecurity.

Insecurity exists in the absence of knowledge. All security derives from knowledge.

One *knows* he will be cared for no matter what happens. That is a security. In the absence of certain knowledge it could also be a fallacy.[18]

Luck is chance. To depend upon luck is to depend upon not-knowingness.

But in truth, how could one have knowledge about life when life itself had not been brought, as knowledge, into order? When the subject of life itself was a chaos, how could work, as a part of life, be anything but a chaos?

If *livingness*[19] is an unknown subject, then *workingness* and all pertaining to work must be an unknown subject, exposed to cynicism, hopelessness and guesses.

To obtain, hold and improve a job, one would have to know the exact, precision rules of life if one were to have a complete

---

18. **fallacy:** a deceptive, misleading or false notion, belief, etc.

19. **livingness:** the activity of going along a certain course, impelled (driven) by a purpose and with some place to arrive.

security. It would not be enough to know, fairly well, one's job. That would not be a security, for as time went on we would see, as we have listed, too many chances entering into it.

Knowledge of the general underlying rules of life would bring about a security of life. Knowledge of the underlying rules of life would also bring about a security in a job.

Scientology is a science of life. It is the first entirely Western effort to understand life. All earlier efforts came from Asia or eastern Europe. And they failed. None of them gave greater security. None of them could change human behavior for the better. None of them—and they bragged about it—could change human intelligence. Scientology is something new under the sun, but young as it is, it is still the only completely and thoroughly tested and validated science of existence. It doesn't demand twenty years of sitting on spikes to find out one is mortal. It doesn't demand a vast study of rats to know that man is confused.

Scientology can and does change human behavior for the better. It puts the individual under the control of himself—where he belongs. Scientology can and does increase human intelligence. By the most exact tests known, it has been proven that Scientology can greatly increase intelligence in an individual. And Scientology can do other things. It can reduce reaction time and it can pull the years off one's appearance. But there is no intention here to give a list of all it can do. It is a science of life and it works. It adequately handles the basic rules of life and it brings order into chaos.

A science of life would be, actually, a science of good order. Such things as accidents and luck would, if you could but understand their underlying principles, be under your control.

As we have seen here, even those who aren't cynical can see

that many chances enter into obtaining, holding and improving one's job. Some of these chances seem so wide and out of control that nothing at all could be done about them. If we could but reduce the chanciness of a job; if we could make the right friends and be sure that our education would count and have some slight security that our interest and intelligence and native ability would not go all to waste, why then, things would be better, wouldn't they?

Well, we'll see what Scientology can do to reduce the chanciness of the workaday world—for you and for those you know. What's life all about anyway?

2

Handling the Confusions of the Workaday World

2

Handling the Confusions of the Workaday World

We have seen how one might be led to believe there was something confusing about navigating one's career in the world of work. And confusion there is to one who is not equipped with guides and maps.

Basically, it all seemed very simple, this thing called work, getting a job. One was educated into some skill and one read an ad, or was sent by a friend and was interviewed for a job. And one got it and then reported every day and did the things assigned and as time went on, hoped for a raise in pay. And time, going even further on, brought one to hope for a pension or a governmental regime[1] that would pay old age benefits. And that was the simple pattern of it.

But times change and simple patterns have a habit of being deranged. The various incidents and accidents of fate entered into the picture. Completely aside from personal factors, larger views alter things. The government in sweeping economy fails to grant adequate pension. The business for which one works is

---

1. **regime:** a form or manner of government or rule.

shattered by a time of depression.[2] Or one's health fails inexplicably and one is left on charity.

The worker in his workaday world is no towering giant amongst his many foes. The tinsel[3] path sketched so happily by rabble-rousers,[4] the great affection held for the worker by this or that ideology[5] or political figure, do not reflect fact. A man working at a job is faced by difficulties large enough to him, no matter how small they might seem to a successful industrialist. A few percent rise in taxes may mean that he thereafter goes without tobacco. An entrance upon bad times for the business may result in lessened pay, and there may go any and all luxuries and even some necessities, or the job.

The effect of international currents, governments, business trends and markets—all usually beyond his concern—the worker is perfectly entitled to believe that his fate is not quite entirely predictable. Indeed, he might even be entitled to be confused.

A man can starve to death in a few days. Few workers have many days of margin in their pockets if the currents change. Thus many things which would be no vast problem to the very secure are watched as menaces by the worker. And these things can become so many that all life seems too confused to be borne and one sinks into an apathy of day-to-day grind, without much hope, trusting that the next storm, by luck, will pass over him.

As one looks at the many factors which might derange his

2. **depression:** a period during which business, employment and stock market values decline severely and remain at a very low level of activity.

3. **tinsel:** showy; gaudy.

4. **rabble-rousers:** persons who try to arouse people to violent action by appeals to emotions, prejudices, etc.

5. **ideology:** the principal ideas or beliefs that characterize a particular class, group or movement.

life and undermine his security, the impression is, confusion seems well founded and it can be said with truth that all difficulties are fundamentally confusions. Given enough menace, enough unknown, a man ducks his head and tries to swing through it blindly. He has been overcome by confusions.

Enough unsolved problems add up to a huge confusion. Every now and then, on his job, enough conflicting orders bring the worker into a state of confusion. A modern plant can be so poorly managed that the entire thing appears to be a vast confusion to which no answer is possible.

Luck is the usual answer one resorts to in a confusion. If the forces about one seem too great, one can always "rely on his luck." By luck we mean "destiny not personally guided." When one turns loose of an automobile wheel and hopes the car will stay on the road by luck, he is often disappointed. And so it is in life. Those things left to chance become less likely to work themselves out. One has seen a friend shutting his eyes to the bill collectors and gritting his teeth while he hopes that he will win at the races and solve all his problems. One has known people who handled their lives this way for years. Indeed, one of Dickens's[6] great characters had the entire philosophy of "waiting for something to turn up." But luck, while we grant that it *is* a potent element, is only necessary amid a strong current of confusing factors. If one has to have *luck* to see him through, then it follows that one isn't any longer at his own automobile wheel and it follows, too, that one is dealing with a confusion.

A confusion can be defined as any set of factors or circumstances which do not seem to have any immediate solution. More broadly, a confusion in this universe is *random motion*.

---

6. **Dickens, Charles:** (1812–70) English novelist of the late nineteenth century whose books are noted for picturesque and extravagant characters in the lower economic strata of England at that time.

If you were to stand in heavy traffic you would be likely to feel confused by all the motion whizzing around you. If you were to stand in a heavy storm, with leaves and papers flying by, you would be likely to be confused.

Is it possible to actually understand a confusion? Is there any such thing as an "anatomy of confusion"? Yes, there is.

If, as a switchboard operator, you had ten calls hitting your board at once, you might feel confused. But is there any answer to the situation? If, as a shop foreman, you have three emergencies and an accident all at the same time, you might feel confused. But is there any answer to that?

A confusion is only a confusion so long as *all* particles are in motion. A confusion is only a confusion so long as no factor is clearly defined or understood.

Confusion is the basic cause of stupidity. To the stupid all things except the very simple ones are confused. Thus if one knew the anatomy of confusion, no matter how bright one might be, he would be brighter.

If you have ever had to teach some young aspirant[7] who was not too bright, you will understand this well. You attempt to explain how such and so works. You go over it and over it and over it. And then you turn him loose and he promptly makes a complete botch of it. He "didn't understand," he "didn't grasp it." You can simplify your understanding of his misunderstanding by saying, very rightly, "He was confused."

Ninety-nine percent of all education fails, when it fails, on the grounds that the student was confused.

---

7. **aspirant:** a person who has ambition toward something.

And not only in the realm of the job, but in life itself, when failure approaches, it is borne, one way or another, from confusion. To learn of machinery or to live life, one has to be able either to stand up to confusion or to take it apart.

We have in Scientology a certain doctrine[8] about confusion. It is called the Doctrine of the Stable Datum.

If you saw a great many pieces of paper whirling about a room, they would look confused until you picked out *one* piece of paper to be the piece of paper by which everything else was in motion. In other words, a confusing motion can be understood by conceiving one thing to be motionless.

In a stream of traffic all would be confusion unless you were to conceive one car to be motionless in relation to the other cars and so to see others in relation to the one.

The switchboard operator receiving ten calls at once solves the confusion by labeling, correctly or incorrectly, one call as the first call to receive her attention. The confusion of ten calls all at once becomes less confusing the moment she singles out one call to be answered. The shop foreman confronted by three emergencies and an accident needs only to elect his *first* target of attention to start the cycle of bringing about order again.

Until one selects *one* datum, *one* factor, *one* particular[9] in a confusion of particles, the confusion continues. The *one* thing selected and used becomes the *stable datum* for the remainder.

---

8. **doctrine:** something taught; teachings.

9. **particular:** a single thing among a number considered by itself; an individual thing or article.

Any body of knowledge, more particularly and exactly, is built from *one datum*. That is its *stable datum*. Invalidate[10] it and the entire body of knowledge falls apart. A stable datum does not have to be the correct one. It is simply the one that keeps things from being in a confusion and on which others are aligned.[11]

Now, in teaching a young aspirant to use a machine, he failed to grasp your directions, if he did, because he lacked a stable datum. *One fact* had to be brought home to him first. Grasping that, he could grasp others. One is stupid, then, or confused in any confusing situation until he has fully grasped *one fact* or one item.

Confusions, no matter how big and formidable they may seem, are composed of data or factors or particles. They have pieces. Grasp one piece and locate it thoroughly. Then see how the others function in relation to it and you have steadied the confusion and, relating other things to what you have grasped, you will soon have mastered the confusion in its entirety.

In teaching a boy to run a machine, don't throw a torrent of data at him and then point out his errors: that's confusion to him, that makes him respond stupidly. Find some entrance point to his confusion, *one datum*. Tell him, "This is a machine." It may be that all the directions were flung at someone who had no real certainty, no real order of existence. "This is a machine," you say. Then make him sure of it. Make him feel it, fiddle with it, push at it. "This is a machine," tell him. And you'd be surprised how long it may take, but you'd be surprised as well how his certainty increases. Out of all the complexities he must learn

---

10. **invalidate:** refute or degrade or discredit or deny something someone else considers to be fact.

11. **aligned:** placed in line, brought into line.

---

to operate it, he must know *one datum* first. It is not even important *which* datum he first learns well, beyond that it is better to teach him a *simple basic datum.* You can show him what it does, you can explain to him the final product, you can tell him why *he* has been selected to run this machine. *But* you *must* make one basic datum clear to him or else he will be lost in confusion.

Confusion is uncertainty. Confusion is stupidity. Confusion is insecurity. When you think of uncertainty, stupidity and insecurity, think of confusion and you'll have it down pat.[12]

What, then, is certainty? Lack of confusion. What then is intelligence? Ability to handle confusion. What then is security? The ability to go through or around or to bring order to confusion. Certainty, intelligence and security are lack of, or ability to handle, confusion.

How does luck fit into confusion? Luck is the hope that some uncontrolled chance will get one through. Counting on luck is an abandonment of control. That's apathy.

There is *good* control and *bad* control. The difference between them is certainty and uncertainty. Good control is certain, positive, predictable. Bad control is uncertain, variable and unpredictable. With good control one can be certain, with bad control one is never certain. A foreman who makes a rule effective today but not tomorrow, who makes George obey but not James, is exercising bad control; in that foreman's wake will come uncertainty and insecurity, no matter what his personal attributes may be.

Because there can be so much uncertain, stupid control, some of us begin to believe that all control is bad. But this is very

12. **have it down pat:** to know or have memorized thoroughly..

far from true. Control is necessary if one would bring any order into confusions. One must be able to control things, his body, his thoughts, at least to some degree, to do anything whatever.

A confusion could be called an *uncontrolled randomness*.[13] Only those who can exert some control over that randomness can handle confusions. Those who cannot exert control actually breed confusions.

The difference between good and bad control then becomes more obvious. The difference between good and bad here is *degree*. A thorough, positive control can be predicted by others. Therefore it is good control. A nonpositive, sloppy control cannot be predicted; therefore it is a bad control. Intention[14] also has something to do with control. Control can be used for constructive purposes or destructive purposes; but you will discover that when destructive purposes are *intended*, bad control is used.

Thus there is a great deal to this entire subject of *confusion*. You may find it rather odd for confusion itself to be used here as a target. But you will find that it is an excellent common denominator to all that we consider evil in life. And if one can become master of confusions, his attention is freed for constructive activity. So long as one is being confused by confusions, all he can think about are destructive things—what he wants to do most is to destroy the confusion.

So let us then learn first how to destroy confusions. And this, we find, is a rather simple thing. When *all* particles seem to be in motion, halt one and see how the others move according to

---

13. **randomness:** condition of being without definite aim, purpose or method, or adherence to a prior arrangement; existing in a haphazard way.

14. **intention:** something that one wishes to do. It is an impulse toward something, an idea that one is going to accomplish something. It is intentional, which means one *means* to do it.

it and then you will find less confusion present. With one adopted as a *stable datum* others can be made to fall in line. Thus an emergency, a machine, a job or life itself can be viewed and understood and one can be free.

Let us take a glance at how this works. In the first chapter we listed a number of things which might influence obtaining, holding and improving a job. One can handle this entire problem, as people most often do, by entering into the problem the single datum, "I can get and hold a job." By clutching to this as a single belief, the confusions and insecurities of life become less effective, less confusing.

But suppose one has done this: Suppose that without further investigating the problem, one, when young, gritted his teeth and shut his eyes and said, "I can get and hold a job, come what may. Therefore I am not going to worry about the economics of existence anymore." Well, that was fine.

Later on, without warning, one got fired. One was out of work for ten weeks. He felt then, even when he did get a new job, less secure, less confident. And let us say that some accident occurred and one was out of a job again. When once more unemployed, he was once more even less confident, less secure. Why?

Let us take a look at the opposite side of this Doctrine of the Stable Datum. If we do, we learn that confusions are held ineffective by stable data and that, when the stable datum is shaken, the confusion comes into being again.

Let us envision a confusion as stopped. It is still scattered but it is stopped. What stopped it? The adoption of a stable datum. Let us say that one was bothered badly in the home by a mother-in-law. One day, after a quarrel, one stalked out and by

inspiration[15] said to himself, "All mothers-in-law are evil." That
was a decision. That, rightly or wrongly, was a stable datum
adopted in a confusion. At once one felt better. He could deal
with or live with the problem now. He knew that "all mothers-
in-law" were evil. It wasn't true, but it was a stable datum. Then
one day, when he was in trouble, his mother-in-law stepped
forward, true-blue,[16] and paid not only the rent but the other
debt, too. At once he felt very confused. This act of kindness
should not have been a thing to bring in confusion. After all,
hadn't she solved the problem? Then why does one feel upset
about it? *Because the stable datum has been shaken.* The entire
confusion of the past problem came into action again by reason
of the demonstrated falsity of the stable datum.

To make anyone confused, all you have to do is locate their
stable data and invalidate them. By criticism or proof it is only
necessary to shake these few stable data to get all a person's
confusions back into action.

You see, stable data do not have to be true. They are simply
adopted. When adopted, then one looks at other data in relation
to them. Thus the adoption of *any* stable datum will tend to
nullify the confusion addressed. *But* if that stable datum is
shaken, invalidated, disproven, then one is left again with the
confusion. Of course, all one has to do is adopt a new stable
datum or put the old stable datum back in place, but he'd have
to know Scientology in order to accomplish this smoothly.

Let us say one has no fears of national economy because of
a heroic political figure who is trying his best. That man is the
stable datum to all one's confusions about national economy.

15. **inspiration:** the fact or condition of being animated or influenced by a feeling,
idea, impulse, etc.

16. **true-blue:** unwaveringly faithful or loyal.

Thus one "isn't worried." But one day circumstances or his political enemies shake him as a datum. They "prove" he was really dishonest. One then becomes worried all over again about national economy. Maybe you adopted some philosophy because the speaker seemed such a pleasant chap. Then some person carefully proves to you that the speaker was actually a thief or worse. One adopted the philosophy because one needed some peace from his thoughts. Invalidating the speaker would then at once bring back the confusion one faced originally.

All right. We looked at the confusion of the workaday world when we were young and we held it all back by stating grimly, "I can get and keep a job." That was the stable datum. We did get a job. But we got fired. The confusion of the workaday world then became very confusing. If we have only the one stable datum, "I can get and keep a job," as our total answer to all the various problems listed in the first chapter, then, assuredly, one is going to spend some confusing periods in his working life. A far, far better stable datum would be, "I understand about life and jobs. Therefore I can get, hold and improve them." And that's where we are going in this book.

3

Is Work Necessary?

3

Is Work
Necessary?

An understanding of life is necessary to the living of it. Otherwise life becomes a trap. To so many of us in the workaday world this trap takes the form of *work*.

If only we didn't have to work, how many delightful things could we do! If only we had some other way of getting money . . . travel, vacations, new clothes . . . what a host of things would be ours if only we didn't have to work!

It is almost an educational factor of our society that work, duress of, is the root of our unhappiness. We hear unions and welfare states as well as individuals basing all their plea upon a reduction of work. Getting rid of work by virtue of reduced hours and the introduction of automatic machinery has become the byword of the mid-twentieth century.

Yet the most disheartening thing which could happen to most of us would be the loss of all future jobs. To be denied the right to work is to be denied any part of the society in which we live.

The rich man's son, the moneyed dowager,[1] neither of them works. Neither is sane. When we look for neurosis and folly in our society we look toward those who do not or cannot work. When we look over the background of a criminal we look at "inability to work." Somehow the right to work seems to be bound up in happiness and the zest of living. And demonstrably the denial of work is bound up with madness and insanity.

As the amount of automatic machinery increases in our society, so increases the percentile[2] of our people who are insane. Child labor laws, injunctions against overtime, demands for many papers and skills and conditions of being, alike combine to reduce the amount of work that can be done by an individual.

Have you ever seen a retired man who pined[3] for his desk? Today "the doctrine of limited work" educates us to believe that at such and such an age we must stop work. Why is this so popular when we can see for ourselves that the end of work is the end of life in most cases?

Speaking politically for a moment, from the standpoint of sanity, man more dearly needs the right to work than he does an endless number of pretended freedoms. Yet we carefully discourage in our children and in our society those people who *make* work. Unless work is made there will be no work to do. Work is not something which springs ready-made into our sight. Work is something that is created. New inventions, new markets, new systems of distribution must be created and brought into existence as times change and old methods, old markets, old systems become inadequate and wear out. Somebody created the jobs we

---

1. **dowager:** a widow with a title or property derived from her dead husband.
2. **percentile:** percentage.
3. **pined:** felt an intense longing.

do. When we work we either do a job created b[...] another.

It is not enough to coast along in a job. The job, [...] has to be made by us, no matter who created it in the first pla[...]

To work is to participate in the activities of our society. To be refused a part in the activities of our society is to be cast out by it.

Somebody invented the difference between work and play. Play was seen to be something that was interesting and work was seen to be something that was arduous[4] and necessary and therefore not interesting. But when we have our vacations and go and "play" we are usually very glad to get back to the "daily grind." Play is almost purposeless. Work has a purpose.

In truth, only the constant refusal on the part of the society to give us work results in our distaste of work when it exists. The man who cannot work was forbidden the right to work. When we go back in the history of the notoriously[5] unable-to-work criminal, we find that he was first and foremost convinced that he must not work—he was forbidden to work whether by his father or mother or school or early life. Part of his education was that he must not work. What was left? Revenge upon the society which refused to let him take part in its activities.

Let us redefine work and play. Play should be called "work without a purpose." It could also be called "activity without purpose." That would make work be defined as "activity with purpose."

Where we have fault to find with working, it grows out of

4. **arduous:** needing much effort; laborious.

5. **notoriously:** talked or known about widely, but in an unfavorable way.

ır own fear that we will not be permitted to continue work.

There is nothing wrong with automation, with all this installation of machines to do our work, so long as the powers that be remember to create *additional work* for us. Automation could be a blessing to the whole world, *providing* as many new jobs are invented as were disposed of by machinery. *Then* we'd have production! And if the powers that be didn't fumble their basic economics and created enough money for us to buy all the new products, *there* would be prosperity indeed. So it isn't automation that is at fault; if automation leaves people unemployed, *somebody* wasn't permitted to invent new jobs for us. Of course, if every new business is flattened by restriction and if every man who would invent work was prohibited from doing so, then and only then would automatic machinery bring about our downfall.

Despite the much-advertised joys of vacations and endless play, such things have never been other than a curse for man. The earliest mention of it was by Homer[6] in the Lotus Isles.[7] And didn't that crew go to pieces!

No, definitely there is more to work and working than having to have a paycheck. Of course there are jobs more interesting than other jobs. Of course there are positions which are more remunerative[8] than other positions. But when one contrasts the right to have a position with *no* right to have one, then one will choose even the less interesting and poorer paid tasks.

Did you know that a mad person could be made well simply

---

6. **Homer:** semilegendary Greek poet of circa eighth century B.C.

7. **Lotus Isles:** also Lotus Lands. In the *Odyssey* by Homer, the hero, Ulysses, and his crew were driven to the land of the Lotus Eaters. These were people who ate the fruit of a plant that caused a man to lose all memory of his homeland and family. Ulysses had to force his crew back to their ship to be able to leave at all.

8. **remunerative:** rewarding; profitable; well-paid.

by getting him convinced that he has some purpose in life? Well, that can happen. It doesn't matter how thin or artificial that purpose may be, mad people can be made sane with it. One instance comes to mind of a crazy girl for whom nothing could be done. That was the point in her case—nothing could be done *for her.* But one night near the asylum an auto accident occurred and an overworked doctor, seeing her near, ordered her to do some things for the victims. She became well. She became a staff nurse. She was never insane thereafter.

Now, no one pretends that we are all mad if we don't work. But it is an astonishing thing that we drift in that direction when we are forbidden to labor.

Great revolutions occur out of a mass inability to work. The crowds rebel not because they are angry over privileges, which they always say, but because they have gone mad, having no work. It is truth that revolutions cannot occur when people are all employed. And it doesn't matter how arduously they are employed either. Revolutions occur when people have been too often forbidden to work. They go up in madness and the state often comes down in ruins. *No* revolution ever won anything. Life evolves into a better condition by means of hard work, not by threats.

If automatic machinery threw enough people out of work— even though the machines were producing aplenty—there would be a revolution. Why? Because by robbing them of work, people have been robbed of a purpose in life. When that goes, all goes.

A good purpose, a bad purpose, it does not matter, so long as a purpose exists. *Why?*

Now, do not think we have strayed very far from the last chapter. We haven't. Here is an understanding of life. Life has certain stable data that *are* the stable data of livingness. Once grasped, then life—and that part of it called work—can be understood.

Life is basically a created thing. But it has many elements in it creating against many other elements in it. A confusion occurs whenever two or more things start creating against each other. Thus life, viewed impartially, can seem to be a confusion.

If one were to sit amongst all this livingness, all this creatingness, all this warfare, without any purpose, his existence in its entirety would be fatal. To be part of a universe, a civilization, and yet to have no purpose, is the route to madness.

The exertion of energy, the exercise, the time spent, the things done are all of a lower order of importance. Just to have *something to do* and a *reason to do it* exerts a control over life itself. If you have no purpose, you have no purchase[9] on the small, first particle necessary to make the whole understandable. Thus life can become a terrible burden.

In the United States in the thirties, and in other lands as well, there was something called a depression. It came out of a lack of understanding of economics during a period of transition into a machine age. During it a great president saw that work had been denied to his people. He created work. He thought he did it to get money into circulation to buy all the things the country could now make. Therefore he did not really rescue the bulk of his people from despair. For the work he gave them was to be carelessly done, poorly done. All that was being demanded was time spent on the job. He had a wonderful opportunity to turn a country into a beautiful thing. But the work given had no purpose.

---

9. **purchase:** a hold or position of advantage for accomplishing something.

Men who detest one job or another detest it because they can't see where it is going or can't believe they are doing any important thing. They are "working"; that is to say, they report and go through motions and draw a paycheck. But they aren't truly a part of the scheme of things. They don't feel they have anything to win.

In our civilization the stable datum to the confusion of existence is *work*. And the stable datum of work is purpose. Even if the purpose is just getting a paycheck, it is still purpose.

Any of us, probably, could do more important things than we are doing. Any of us could use some changes in our tasks. But none of us, and still stay alive and sane, could do without something to do.

When we grow timid in the face of circumstance it is because our purpose, our stable data, have been invalidated.

It is, as we have shown, rather easy to knock a person into a state of confusion. All you have to do is locate his stable datum on any subject and shake it. This is a trick we all use. For instance, we are arguing about economics with a friend: we don't agree with him. We ask him where he got such an idea. He says somebody wrote it in such and so. We attack the writer or the paper and discredit it. In other words, we win our argument by shaking his stable datum as nearly as we can find it.

Life is competitive. Many of us forget we are part of a team called man, in contest with who knows what else to survive. We attack man and attack our friends. In the course of holding a job, it seems only natural that here and there in the organization would be people who were so insecure in their own tasks that they seek to spread insecurity around them.

Having drunk of confusion too deeply, having too few

stable data, a person can begin to dramatize confusion, to spread it, to consciously try to make everything and everybody confused. One of the favorite targets of such people is the stable datum of work. Although usually such people cannot even do their own jobs, they are very anxious to make others tired of theirs. They "cut down their competition" by carving up the stable data of others.

Beware these people who come around and inquire "sympathetically" about your health because you look "overworked." It is almost easier to get "overloafed" than overworked. Beware these people who want you to sign a petition to shorten the hours to be spent on the job. The end product of that is no job. And beware, too, the fellow who is always taking it "out of the firm" because the firm can afford it. Remember, that firm is part yours, no matter if they fire you tomorrow. Such people are trying to pull out from under you the stable datum of work.

If you are afraid of losing your job, it is because you suffer already from too many forbiddings to work. The only way to hold a job is to make it every day, to create it and keep it created. If you have no wish to create and continue that job then there must be something at cross-purposes with purpose. There is something wrong between what you think would be a good purpose and what purpose your job has.

Government jobs are an interesting example because, so often, nobody seems to care really whether the job has purpose or not. Too often the purpose of having a government job is just to have a government job. Here in particular one has to understand about life and work itself, for a government job has to be created continually to continue. And if it seems to have no purpose then one should look over government itself and get at *its* purpose, for the purpose of the government as a whole, in some part, would be the purpose of the job held, no matter how small.

Anyone suffering from a distaste for work must basically have a feeling that he isn't really allowed to work. Thus work is not a stable datum in life. And he must have, as well, some cross-purpose about the purposes of his job. And, too, he usually is associated with people in his job who are trying to make work into something less than tasteful. But he is to be pitied because he is unhappy. He is unhappy because he is confused. Why is he confused? Because he has no stable datum for his life. And a stable datum for life itself is the basis of good living as well as good job orientation.

4

The Secret
of Efficiency

4

The Secret of Efficiency[1]

What is control?

Whether one handles a machine of the size of a car or as small as a typewriter or even an accounting pen, one is faced with the problems of control. An object is of no use to anyone if it cannot be controlled. Just as a dancer must be able to control his body, so must a worker in an office or a factory be able to control his body, the machines of his work and, to some degree, the environment around him.

The primary difference between "the worker" in an office or a factory and an executive is that the executive controls minds, bodies and the placement of communications, raw materials and products, and the worker controls, in the main, his immediate tools. However, it is far too easy for those anxious to agitate labor into measures not necessarily good for it, and for executives who themselves are anxious for control and anxious about it, to forget that the worker who does not control his materials of work and who is himself a controlled factor only, is practically useless to the plant itself. Both management and labor must be able to

---

1. **efficiency:** accomplishment of or ability to accomplish a job with a minimum expenditure of time and effort.

control their immediate environment. The most apparent difference between an executive and a "worker" is that the executive controls more environment than the "worker." To that degree, then, the executive must be more capable than the "worker" or the plant or business is doomed to difficulty if not failure.

What is a good workman? He is one who can positively control his equipment or tools of trade or who can control the communication lines[2] with which he is intimately connected.

What is a bad worker? A bad worker is one who is unable to control the equipment he is supposed to control or the communication lines he is supposed to handle.

People who wish to control others, but who do not wish others to control anything, bring us into a difficulty by establishing a fallacy. That fallacy is that there is such a thing as "bad" control. Control is either well done or not done. If a person is controlling something he is controlling it. If he is controlling it poorly he is not controlling it. A machine which is being run well is controlled. A machine which is not being run well is not being controlled. Therefore we see that bad control is actually a not-control.

People who tell you that control is bad are trying to tell you that automobile accidents and industrial accidents are good.

Attempted control for bad or covert purposes is harmful and it carries with it the ingredient of unknowingness. The person who is *attempting* control is actually not controlling. He is simply seeking to control and his efforts are, in the main, indefinite and

---

2. **communication lines:** routes along which communication travels from one person to another; any sequences through which a message of any character may go.

unpositive,[3] which of course are characteristics which control itself does not countenance.[4] When unknowingness is entered into control, control can become antipathetic, but it does not become a fact. If you have ever covertly controlled your car you will understand what is meant. If you handled your steering wheel in such a way that the car would not "know" which way it was then supposed to go, you would soon be involved in difficulties. You must handle the steering wheel of a car in such a way that the car then turns the proper turns and remains on a straight course on a straight road. There is nothing hidden about your intention of controlling the car and there is nothing unknown about the response of the car. When a car fails to respond to your handling of the steering wheel, control has ceased to exist.

In other words, one either controls something or he does not. If he does not we have developed a misnomer. We have developed the idea there is such a thing as bad control.

People who have been "badly controlled," which is to say, who have been merely shaken up and have not been controlled at all, begin to believe that there is something bad about control, but they would really not know what control is since they have not been controlled in actuality.

To understand this further one would have to know one of the very basic principles of Scientology, which is the anatomy of control. In part this principle consists as follows: Control may be subdivided into three separate parts. These parts are *start*, *change* and *stop*.

Start, change and stop also comprise a cycle of action. The

---

3. **unpositive:** not precise; not specific.

4. **countenance:** support, approve or tolerate.

---

cycle of action is seen in the turning of a simple wheel. The wheel starts and then any given spot on it changes position and then the wheel is stopped. It does not matter how long the wheel is in motion, it still follows this cycle of action. A man walking a short distance starts, changes the position of his body and stops his body. He has, if he does this, completed a cycle of action. On a longer span a company starts, continues and at some date, early or late, ceases to exist. In change we get change of position in space or change of existence in time. In start we have simply start and in stop we have simply stop. Things may start slowly or rapidly, things may stop slowly or rapidly, things may change very rapidly while they are going. Thus the rate of start, the rate of change and the rate of stop have little to do with the fact that a cycle of action does consist of start, change and stop.

The ancients referred to this cycle of action in a much more detailed fashion. We find the Vedic hymns[5] talking about a cycle of action in this wise: First there is chaos; then from the chaos something emerges and can be said to have been born; it grows, it persists, it decays and dies and chaos ensues. Although this in essence is an inaccurate statement, it is the earliest example of a cycle of action.

A modern Scientology example of a cycle of action is much more simply stated and is much more accurate. A cycle of action is start, change and stop. This parallels another cycle of action which is that of life itself. The cycle of action of life is *creation, survival* and *destruction*. Survival could be said to be any change, whether in size or in age or in position in space. The essence of survival is change. Creation is of course starting, destruction is of course stopping. Thus we have in Scientology two very useful cycles of action: The first of them being start, change and stop

---

5. **Vedic hymns:** the sacred books of the Hindus. These were religious hymns comprising some 125,000–150,000 volumes.

---

and the more detailed one being create, survive, destroy.

Start, change and stop imply the conditions of a being or an object. Create, survive, destroy imply the intention of life toward objects.

Control consists entirely of starting, changing and stopping. There are no other factors in positive control. If one can start something, change its position in space or existence in time and stop it, all at will, he can be said to control it, whatever it may be. If one can barely manage to start something, can only with difficulty continue its change of position or existence in time, and if one can only doubtfully stop something, he cannot be said to control it well, and for our purposes he would be said to be able to control it poorly or dangerously. If he cannot start something, if he cannot change its position in space, if he cannot stop something, then he is definitely not in control of it. If he is trying to start, change and stop something or somebody without positively doing so, he has entered unknowingness into the activity and the result will be questionable to say the least.

Thus there is such a thing as good control. Good control would consist of knowingness and positiveness. A girl who can start a typewriter, continue its motion and then stop it could be said to be in control of the typewriter. If she had difficulties in starting it, in continuing its action and in stopping it, she would not only be in "bad control" of the typewriter, she would be a bad stenographer.

Where "bad control" enters in, so enter incompetence, accidents, difficulties, disobedience, inefficiency and, not the least, considerable misery and unhappiness. As we define bad control as not-control, or as an unknowing attempt at control without actually effecting control, it can be said that unpositiveness results in a great many difficulties.

To give you some idea of how far this might go in life, you might get the idea of being moved around in a room by somebody. This somebody would tell you to go to the desk, then would tell you to go to a chair, then would tell you to go to the door. Each time he tells you to go somewhere, you of course have to start yourself, change your body's position and stop yourself. Now, oddly enough, you would not mind this if you knew that somebody was telling you to do it and you were capable of performing the action and you were not receiving orders in such a wise as to interrupt your obedience of the command before you completed it. Let us say, for instance, that somebody told you to go to the desk, but before you arrived at the desk he told you to go to a chair, but before you arrived at the chair told you to go to the door and then claimed you were wrong in not having gone to the desk. You would be, at that time, confused. This would be "bad control" since it does not permit you to finish any cycle of action before another cycle of action is demanded of you. Thus your cycles of action become involved[6] and a confusion results. But this, in essence, would not be control since control must involve an understandable or knowing positiveness. Good control would not change the order before you had a chance to arrive at the desk. It would let you arrive at the desk before you were asked to start again for the chair. It would let you arrive at the chair before you were asked to start again for the door. Now, you would not mind the positive control, but it is certain that you would be quite upset by the broken series of orders which did not permit you to finish any cycle of action. Now, to give you some idea of how this could influence one's life—which would you rather have give you a series of orders such as above, to move around a room: your father or your mother? It is certain that you had the most trouble with the parent you would not have chosen to have given you those orders.

6. **involved:** complicated.

Control is so far from being bad that a person who is sane and in very good condition does not resent good, positive control and is himself able to administer good, positive control to people and objects. A person who is not in very good condition resents even the most casual directions and is actually not capable of controlling people or objects. The latter person is also inefficient and has many difficulties with work and with life.

When a person cannot control things or when he resists things controlling him, he involves himself with difficulties not only with people but with objects. It is also apparent that people with control difficulties more readily become ill and fail in other ways.

When a person is incapable of controlling a piece of machinery it often occurs that the machinery reverses the matter and begins to control him. As an example, a driver who cannot exert positive control on a car is quite likely, eventually, to be controlled by that car. Instead of a driver driving a car down the street, we have a car taking a "driver" down the street and sooner or later the car, not being very expert at control, winds its driver up in a ditch.

Even mechanical failures are attributable to a lack of control. It will be discovered that an individual who cannot easily control a machine is quite likely to have considerable difficulties with that machine. The machine itself suffers sometimes in nearly inexplicable ways. Motors run for some men and do not run for others. Some machinery will go on for years in the hands of a mechanic, but when the mechanic leaves it and another takes his place who is not adept,[7] the machine may be found to break down and experience difficulties never before noticed in it. It is stretching things a little bit to infer that a person who cannot

---

7. **adept:** highly skilled; expert.

control things needs only to look at a piece of machinery to have something go wrong with it, and yet there are cases on record where this has happened. The factor involved is more easily understood in, for instance, an accounting department. A person who cannot control figures, of course, sooner or later involves the books he is keeping in complexities and intricacies which not even an expert accountant can straighten out.

The cycle of action of this universe is start, change and stop. This is also the anatomy of control. Almost the entire subject of control is summed up in the ability to start, change and stop one's activities, body and his environment.

A habit is simply something one cannot stop. Here we have an example of no control whatever and we have the step beyond the last extremity of entirely lost control. Control begins to dwindle when one is able to change things and stop things but is not still capable of starting them. Once a thing is started, such a person can change and stop it. A further dwindling of control, if one can now call it such, would be the loss of an ability to change something or continue its existence in time. This would leave one simply with the ability to stop things. When one finally loses the ability to stop something, that thing has to some degree become his master.

In the *stop* of start, change and stop we see, in essence, the entirety of the stable datum. If one can stop just one particle or datum in a confusion of particles or data one has begun a control of that confusion. In the matter of a mass of calls coming into a switchboard simultaneously, each call insistently demanding the attention of an operator, control is asserted on the switchboard by the operator's stopping just one demand. It does not particularly matter which demand is stopped. Handling just one call permits one then to handle another call and so forth until one has changed the condition of the switchboard from a total confusion to a handled situation. One feels confused when there is nothing in a situation which he can stop. When he can at least stop one thing in a situation, he will then find it is possible to stop others and finally will recover the ability to change certain factors in the situation. From this he graduates into an ability to change anything in the situation and finally is capable of starting some line of action.

Control is then found to be very intimate to confusion. A worker who is easily confused is a worker who cannot control things. An executive who is frantic in the face of an emergency is an executive who, even in good times, does not feel that he has any ability to actually start, change and stop situations in which he is involved as an executive.

Franticness, helplessness, incompetence, inefficiency and other undesirable factors in a job are all traceable to inabilities to start, change and stop things.

Let us say that a plant has a good manager. The manager can start, change and stop the various activities in which the plant is involved; can start, change and stop the various machinery of the plant; can start, change and stop the raw materials and the products of the plant; and can start, change and stop various labor activities or difficulties. But let us say that this plant is unfortunate enough to have only one person in it who can start, change and stop things. Now unless the executive is going to handle all the incoming raw materials, turn on and off all the machinery, process every piece of material in the place and ship the finished products himself, he will be unable to run the plant. Similarly an office manager who himself can start, change and stop any of the activities of an office or handle them, if he were the only one in the office who could, would be powerless actually to run a very large office.

In a plant or in an office it is then necessary for an executive, no matter how good he may be, to be supported by subordinates who themselves are not unwilling to be started, changed and stopped by him, but who can themselves start, change and stop the activities or personnel in their own immediate environments in the plant.

Now given a good executive in a plant or office and given good subordinates (defining as good, their ability to start, change and stop things), we would yet have difficulty if we reached lower down on the command chart and discovered that we did not have any working people who themselves were capable of starting, changing and stopping their own particular jobs. We would have a condition here where the executive and the foreman would then be forced to do everything that was really being done in the plant. To actually have a good plant we would have to have an executive, foreman and workers, all of whom in their own environment were capable of starting, changing and stopping things and who were at the same time (including the executives) not unwilling to be started, changed and stopped in their duties, providing positive and understandable orders were used.

As we look this over we see less and less the picture we have been uniformly presented with in plants and offices of the "management" and "laborers." As soon as we discover one worker in a plant who does not have to start, change or stop himself or anything else we would then have somebody who would justify this title of "laborer." It is apparent that from the topmost member of the board down to the lowest worker on the payroll, each and every one of them is involved with starting, changing and stopping people, materials, machinery, products and pieces of the environment. In other words, each and every one of them present in a plant or an office is actually managing something. As soon as an executive realizes this, he is then capable of running a far more efficient business since he is capable, then, of selecting out from amongst them, people who are best at starting, changing and stopping things, and these by example can bring others into a state of mind where they, too, are willing to positively start, change and stop things.

However, in executives, foremen or workers, we have people today who are either stuck on one or another of the factors of control exclusively or who are incapable of any of the factors of control. Thus we have, in any plant or office or business or activity — even the government — a considerable amount of confusion which would not be present if the people there were capable of controlling what they were supposed to control.

We have people in the workaday world, whether managers or janitors, who are for instance fixated (stuck) on starting. These people can start all day and all night but they never get going. Such people talk about big schemes and big deals; such people talk a lot of enthusiasm about getting going but never themselves seem to move.

Others, no matter what their class or classification, get fixated on change. These manifest this usually by insisting that everything "keep running." They talk all the time about "keeping things going," but they will not listen to any new ideas or will not receive any new machinery, since that would necessitate stopping some old machinery and starting some new machinery. Thus we get antiquated plants and systems continued on forever, long past their usefulness or economic value. A subdivision of this is the person who must change everything all the time. This is actually another manifestation of trying to keep things running, but instead of keeping things running, these people shift everything there is to be shifted all the time. If an order is issued they change the order. If they receive the word to go they change it to stay. But this, it will be seen, is an unbalanced

condition where these people are actually unwilling to keep anything running anywhere and are in reality on an obsessive[8] stop.

Plants, businesses, factories, ships and even the government
are victimized particularly by people who can only stop things.
No matter how well some unit may be running, some order is
issued that stops whatever it is doing. It is enough for such
people to discover that something is going to do something to
cause it to stop. Usually one gets around this by failing to inform
such people that something is running.

Thus we can see that there are people who abuse the cycle
of action of start, change and stop and who are themselves
fixated upon one or another factor in the cycle of action or who
are incapable of withstanding any factor in it, which means, of
course, that they are in a continuous and arduous confusion.

It is noteworthy that those people who can only start things
are normally creative. The artist, the writer, the designer, is
looked upon to start things. He actually might also be capable of
continuing them or stopping them, but his purest function is
creation.

There are amongst very rational and good men those whose
greatest ability is continuing things. They can also start things
and stop things if they can really continue things. It is upon
these men that we depend for the survival of a business or an
operation.

Then there is the class that is used by the society to stop
things. Such people have normally a police function. Certain
things are declared to be bad and these things so designated are

---

8. **obsessive:** of or having to do with a persistent drive or urge a person cannot
control.

then turned over to people who stop them. Imperfect production is stopped by inspectors. Bribery, corruption or crime is stopped by police. Other nationally aggressive persons are stopped by the military. And it should occasion[9] no surprise that these specialists in stop are, of course, specializing in destroy. It should occasion no further surprise that when one looks at the element in a society most likely to decay the society, one looks for those whose job it is to specialize in stops. These people, in the main, while serving a very good function for the society at large, if they became fully in charge, as in a police state, would only destroy the state and its people, as has been noted since the days of Napoleon.[10] The most recent nation which turned over the entire function of the state to police was Germany and Germany was stopped very thoroughly. Germany also effected nothing but destruction.

When we have a society which is very good at starting we have a creative society. When we have a society which is very good at keeping things running we have a society that endures. When we have a society that is only capable of stopping things we have a society which is destructive or which is itself destroyed. Therefore, we must realize that a balance amongst these three factors of start, change and stop is necessary not only in an individual but in a business, and not only in a business but in a nation. When one can only do one of these one is considerably limited in his usefulness. The optimum condition would be for everyone from manager down to janitor to be capable of starting, changing and stopping and to be able to endure being started, changed and stopped. Thus we would have a balanced and relatively unconfused business activity.

9. **occasion:** to cause or bring about.

10. **Napoleon Bonaparte:** (1769–1821) French military leader. He rose to power in France by military force, declared himself emperor and conducted campaigns of conquest across Europe until his final defeat by armies allied against him in 1815.

No business can succeed unless it has been properly started, unless it is progressing through time or changing position in space and unless it is capable of stopping harmful practices and even competitors.

As it is with a nation or a business, so it would be with an individual holding down a single job. He should be able to start, change and stop anything under his immediate control. If he is running a machine he should be able to start the machine, to keep it turning (changing) and to stop it, and this should be under his own determinism. His machine should not be started by some engineer and stopped at some period of the day without any attention from himself. Furthermore, if he thought the machine should be shut down and oiled he should have the authority to do so and should not have to withstand the pummeling of some machine foreman who, without understanding the situation, simply observed that a machine was stopped which according to his lights[11] ought to be running.

Even a janitor, to have any efficiency at his job and thus to have a clean set of offices or a plant, would have to be able to start, change and stop the various objects having to do with his particular job. He should not have to keep on sweeping after the floor is clean and he should not have to stop sweeping before he has cleaned the floor and he should be able to start sweeping the floor when he believes it ought to be swept. Naturally, if he is able to do these things he is also able to cooperate with his fellow workers, and himself be stopped or started or altered in his activity, so as to execute his job while making it possible for them to do their jobs.

Here, however, we envision a nation or a plant or an office

---

11. **according to his lights:** following his own ideas, intelligence and conscience in the best way that he knows.

or a small section or department running without any supervision at all, whereas there would be executives and foremen and workers. It is doubtful if supervision of others would occupy much of anyone's time. As the ability of the worker and foreman and executive to start, change and stop those things which they should handle and control declines, it will be discovered that supervision enters in. The less capable people are of starting, changing and stopping the people or objects under their immediate control, the more supervision they require. When supervision gets up to eighty percent of the plant's activities it is certain that the confusion will be so great that inefficiency will result in such magnitude as to ruin the activity.

Supervision, then, is actually a criticism of the junior. It implies that the junior does not know or is not able in the field of control.

Cooperation and alignment of activity is different than supervision. Where one has a chain of command one does not necessarily have supervision. One *does* have, however, coordinated planning for an entire operation which is then relayed to others in the operation so that coordination can take place. If everybody is agreed on the worthwhileness of any activity and if everybody in that activity were capable of actually controlling those items or persons which were in his immediate sphere of action, it would be found that planning would not have to engage in much supervision in order to effect the execution of the ideas involved. This is a very high order of dream. Only where Scientology has been thoroughly at work could such a thing occur—that an organization could run in agreement with itself without supervision or punitive action.

One is able to gauge those workers around him by the amount of confusion in which they are involved. That confusion tells one at once the degree of inability to control things. That inability to control things may not be entirely the fault of the worker. There are two things which can be psychotic: one is the surroundings and the other is the person. A sane man has difficulty in insane surroundings. An insane man has difficulty in even the sanest and most orderly surroundings. Thus there are two factors involved in any operation: the person and the surroundings. It could also be said there are two factors involved in any business: the surroundings of the business itself and the business. One sane business trying to operate in a world of madmen would have a very great difficulty getting along. One way or another the inability of the madmen to start, change and stop things would infect the business and deteriorate its efficiency.

Thus it is not enough that an individual himself be capable of controlling his job. He must also be able to tolerate the confusion of those around him who cannot control their jobs, or he must be able to tolerate sane and steady control from those around him.

Insanity is contagious. Confusion is contagious. Have you ever talked to a confused man without yourself, at the end of the conversation, feeling a little confused? Thus it is in work. If one is working with a great many men who are incapable, one begins himself to feel incapable. It is not enough to live alone. It is impossible to work alone. Realizing this, one also understands that his ability to control the immediate machinery or work tools with which he is involved would also include an ability to assist others in his vicinity to control those things with which they are involved.

Many a good worker has been lost to a factory because the good worker could not make his own work good enough to satisfy himself, being faced in his job with so many confused elements and orders that he at last rebelled. Thus good workers can be spoiled. In any department it is possible to spot the people who spoil good workers. They are the people who cannot start, change and stop such things as communication or machinery and who are themselves most liable to franticness and confusion. These are the people who would rather have solutions thrown in the wastebasket and problems posted on the bulletin board.

What could one do if he was surrounded by people who were confused and incapable of starting, changing and stopping their various activities? He could himself become sufficiently capable at his own job that he would set a fine example for others and thus himself be a stable datum in the confusion of that area. He could do even more than this. He could understand how to handle men and, so understanding, could bring orderliness into the minds and activities of those men so as to balk[12] their inabilities as they might affect him. But in order to do the latter he would have to know a great deal about Scientology and its various principles, and that is somewhat beyond the scope of this particular volume.

For the individual worker who wishes to do a good job and to go on having a job and to rise in his position, it is almost enough that he understand his job thoroughly so that no part of it confuses him and so that he can start, change or stop anything with which he is connected in that job and that he himself can tolerate being started, changed and stopped by his superiors without himself becoming unsettled. In other words, the greatest asset and greatest job insurance a worker could have would be a calmness of mind concerning what he was doing. A calmness of mind is derived from the ability to start, change and stop the objects and activities with which he is involved and to be able to

---

12. **balk:** to obstruct or hinder.

be started, changed and stopped by others without himself becoming as confused as they are.

Thus the secret of doing a good job is the secret of control itself. One not only continues to create a job, day by day, week by week, month by month, he also continues the job by permitting it to progress, and he is also capable of stopping or ending any cycle of work and letting it remain finished.

Workers are most often victimized by bosses, juniors or marital partners who are not themselves capable of controlling anything, yet who will not be controlled and who in some peculiar way are obsessed[13] on the idea of control. A worker who is thus intimately connected with something that he himself cannot control and which is incapable of actually or really controlling him, performs his work in a confused state which can only lead to difficulties and distaste for work itself.

It can be said that the only thing bad about working is that it is so very often associated with inabilities to control. When these are present then the work itself seems tiresome, arduous and uninteresting, and one would rather do anything else than continue that particular work. There are many solutions to this. First amongst them is to regain control of the items or functions which one is most intimately connected with in doing his job.

However, control in itself is not an entire answer to everything, for if it were one would have to be able to control everything, not only in his own job, but in an office or on Earth, before he could be happy. We discover in examining control that the limits of control should be extended only across one's actual sphere of operation. When an individual attempts to extend control far beyond his active interest in a job or in life he

---

13. **obsessed:** haunted or troubled in the mind; preoccupied greatly.

encounters difficulty. Thus there is a limit to the "area of control" which, if violated, violates many things. It is almost a maxim[14] that if an individual consistently seeks to operate outside his own department he will not take care of his own department. As a matter of fact, in Scientology organizations it has been discovered that a person who is consistently involving himself with things far beyond his actual scope of interest is not covering his actual scope of interest. Thus there is obviously another factor involved than control. This factor is willingness not to control and is fully as important as control itself.

14. **maxim:** a concisely expressed principle or rule of conduct, or a statement of a general truth.

5

Life as a Game

5

Life as a Game

It is quite obvious that if anyone controlled everything he would have no game. There would be no unpredictable factors, no surprises in life. This might be said to be a hell of considerable magnitude.

If one could control everything absolutely, he would of course be able to predict everything absolutely. If he could predict the course and action of every motion in the entirety of existence, he would of course have no real interest in it.

We have already looked at the necessity of controlling the immediate objects of work, but remember it is necessary, if one controls these immediate objects, to have other objects or environments which one does not absolutely control. Why is this?

It is because life is a game.

The word *game* is used here advisedly.[1] When one is mired down in the sometimes titanic struggle of existence, he is apt to discount[2] the fact that there is joy in living. He is apt to disbelieve

---

1. **advisedly:** with due consideration; deliberately.
2. **discount:** to disbelieve or disregard entirely; set aside as inaccurate or irrelevant.

that such a thing as fun can exist. Indeed people, when they reach into their thirties, begin to wonder what happened to their childhood when they actually could enjoy things. One begins to wonder if pleasure of living isn't itself some sort of trap, and one begins to believe that it is not a good thing to become too interested in new people and new things, since these will only lead to heartbreak. There are men who have decided that in view of the fact that loss brings so much pain, they had better not acquire at all. It is far superior according to these to live a life of only medium privation[3] than to live a life of considerable luxury, since then if they lost what they had the pain would be much less.

Life, however, is a game. It is very easy to see a game in terms of cricket or football. It is not so easy to see life as a game when one is forced to rise before the sun and reach his home only after it sets, after a day of arduous and relatively unthanked toil. One is likely to dispute that such an activity could be a game at all. Nevertheless, it is obvious in various experiments which have been made in Scientology that life, no matter what its emotional tone[4] or lack of it, is in essence a game and that the elements of life itself are the elements of games.

Any job is a game.

A game consists of freedoms, barriers and purposes. There are many more complicated factors involved in games, but these are all listed in Scientology.

Primary amongst these is the necessity in a game to have an opponent or an enemy. Also a necessity is to have problems.

---

3. **privation:** lack of the ordinary necessities or comforts of life.

4. **emotional tone:** the general condition of an individual. *See also* **Tone Scale** in the glossary.

Another necessity is to have sufficient individuality to cope with a situation. To live life fully, then, one must have, in addition to "something to do," a higher purpose; and this purpose, to be a purpose at all, must have counter-purposes or purposes which prevent it from occurring. One must have individualities which oppose the purpose or activities of one, and if one lacks these things it is certain that he will invent them.

This last is very important. If a person lacks problems, opponents and counter-purposes to his own, *he will invent them.* Here we have in essence the totality of aberration.[5] But more intimately to our purposes we have the difficulties which arise from work.

If we had a foreman who capably controlled everything in his area and did nothing else, and if that foreman were not entirely mentally balanced in all ways (which is to say if he were human), we would find that foreman inventing personalities for the workers under him and reasons why they were opposing him and actual oppositions. We would find him selecting out one or more of his workmen to chastise,[6] with, according to the foreman, very good reason, but in actuality without any further reason than that the foreman obsessively needs opponents. Now, very many involved classifications can be read into this by ancient mental analyses but none of these need to be examined.

---

5. **aberration:** a departure from rational thought or behavior. From the Latin, *aberrare*, to wander from; Latin, *ab*, away, *errare*, to wander. It means basically to err, to make mistakes, or more specifically to have fixed ideas which are not true. The word is also used in its scientific sense. It means departure from a straight line. If a line should go from A to B, and it is "aberrated" it would go from A to some other point, to some other point, to some other point, to some other point, to some other point and finally arrive at B. Taken in its scientific sense, it would also mean the lack of straightness or to see crookedly as, for example, a man sees a horse but thinks he sees an elephant. Aberrated conduct would be wrong conduct, or conduct not supported by reason. Aberration is opposed to sanity which would be its opposite.

6. **chastise:** to scold or condemn sharply.

The truth of the matter is that a man must have a game, and if he does not have one he will make one. If that man is aberrated and not entirely competent, he will make an intensely aberrated game.

Where an executive finds all running far too smoothly in his immediate vicinity, he is likely to cause some trouble just to have something to do—unless that executive is in very good mental condition indeed. Thus we have management pretending, often without any actual basis in fact, that labor is against it. Similarly, we occasionally have labor certain that management, which is in fact quite competent, is against labor. Here we have invented a game where no game can actually exist.

When men become very shortsighted[7] they cannot look actually beyond their own environment. There is in any office, plant or activity the game of the office, plant or activity itself versus its competitors and versus its outer environment. If that office, plant or activity and all the personnel within it are conducting themselves on a wholly rational and effective basis, they choose the outside world and other rival concerns for their game. If they are not up to par[8] and are incapable of seeing the real game, they will make up a game and the game will begin to be played inside the office and inside the plant.

In playing games one has individuals and teams. Teams play against teams; individuals play against individuals. When an individual is not permitted to be fully a part of the team he is apt to choose other members of the team as his opponents for, remember, man *must* have a game.

Out of all these complexities come the various complexities

---

7. **shortsighted:** lacking in foresight.

8. **par:** average or normal state, condition, degree, etc.

of work and the problems of production and communication.

If everybody in a plant were able to control his own sphere of interest in that plant and if everybody in the plant were doing his own job, there would actually be no lack of game, for there are other plants, other activities in the outside world and these always furnish game enough for any rational organization. But supposing the people in an organization cannot control their own sphere, cannot control their own activities, and are obsessively attempting to create aberrated games all about them. Then we would have a condition whereby the plant, office or concern[9] would not be able to effectively fight its environment and would produce poorly, if not collapse.

Aberrated or not aberrated, competent or not competent, remember, life is a game and the motto of any individual or team alive is, "There *must* be a game." If individuals are in good mental and physical condition they actually play the game which is obvious and in plain sight. If they are not in good condition and if they are themselves incapable of controlling their own immediate environment, they will begin to play games with their tools. Here the machinist will find his machine suddenly incapable of producing. One would not go so far as to say that he will actually break the machine so that he can have a game with it, but he will be in a mild state of fury regarding that machinery continually. The bookkeeper, unable to control his immediate tools of trade and not well fitted into his concern, will begin to play a game with his own figures and will fail to get balances. His adding machine will break down, his papers will get lost and other things will occur under his immediate nose which never should happen, and if he were in good shape and could play the actual game of keeping other people in the plant straight so far as their accounts and figures are concerned, he would be efficient.

---

9. **concern:** a business establishment.

Efficiency, then, could be defined as the ability to play the game to hand. Inefficiency could be defined as an inability to play the game to hand, with a necessity to invent games with things which one should actually be able to control with ease.

This sounds almost too simple, but unfortunately for the professors that try to make things complicated, it is just that simple. Of course there are a number of ways men can become aberrated. That is not the subject of this book. The subject of this book is work.

Now, realizing that life *must* be a game, one should realize that there is a limit to the area one would control and still retain an interest in life. Interest is mainly kindled by the unpredictable. Control is important. Uncontrol is, if anything, even more important. To actually handle a machine perfectly one must be *willing* to control it or not to control it. When control itself becomes obsessive we begin to find things wrong with it. The individual who absolutely has to control everything in sight is upsetting to all of us and this individual is why we have begun to find things wrong with control. It sounds very strange to say that uncontrol must also be under control, but this is, in essence, true. One must be *willing* to leave certain parts of the world uncontrolled. If he cannot, he rapidly drops downscale[10] and gets into a situation where he is obsessively attempting to control things which he never will be able to control and thus renders himself unhappy, begins to doubt his ability to control those things which he actually should be able to control and so at length loses his ability to control anything. And this, in essence, is what in Scientology we call the dwindling spiral of control.

There are mental factors which we will not discuss here, which tend to accumulate the failures to control to a point where

---

10. **downscale:** into the lower-level emotions, such as apathy, anger, etc.

one is no longer confident of his ability to control. The truth of the matter is an individual actually desires to have some part of life uncontrolled. When this part of life hurts him sufficiently, he then resigns himself to the necessity of controlling it and so makes himself relatively unhappy if he never will be able to do so.

A game consists of freedoms, barriers and purposes. It also consists of control and uncontrol.

An opponent in a game *must* be an uncontrolled factor. Otherwise one would know exactly where the game was going and how it would end and it would not be a game at all.

Where one football team would be totally capable of control-ling the other football team, we have no football game. This is a matter of no contest. There would be no joy or sport in playing that game of football. Now, if a football player has been seriously injured playing football, a new unknowing factor enters into football for *him*. This injury lodges in what we call the *reactive mind*.[11] It is a mind which is unseen and which works all the time. One normally works on what we call the *analytical mind*[12] and this we know all about. Anything that we have forgotten or moments of unconsciousness and pain become locked away in the reactive mind and are then capable of *reacting* upon the individual in such a way as to make him refrain from doing something which was once dangerous. While this is a rather

---

11. **reactive mind:** the portion of the mind which works on a stimulus-response basis (given a certain stimulus it will automatically give a certain response) which is not under a person's volitional control and which exerts force and power over a person's awareness, purposes, thoughts, body and actions.

12. **analytical mind:** the conscious, aware mind which thinks, observes data, remembers it, and resolves problems. It would be essentially the conscious mind as opposed to the unconscious mind. In Scientology, the analytical mind is the one which is alert and aware and the reactive mind simply reacts without analysis.

technical subject, it is nevertheless necessary to understand that one's past has a tendency to accumulate and victimize one in the future. Thus, in the case of the football player, while he plays football he is apt to be *restimulated*[13] or *react from* the old injury received in football and so feels less than a spirit of fun while playing football. He becomes anxious. He becomes very grim on the subject of football and this is expressed by an effort to actively control the players on another team so that they will not injure him again.

In a motorcycle race a famous motorcycle rider was injured. Two weeks later in another race we find this motorcycle rider falling out on the fifth lap without injury or incident but simply pulling over into the pits. He did this immediately after a motorcycle swerved close to him. He recognized at once that he was unable to control that motorcycle. He felt then incapable of controlling his own motorcycle and so knew one thing—he had to get out of that race. And just as this motorcycle rider abandoned that race, so all of us at one time or another have abandoned sections of life.

Now, up to the time he had that accident the motorcycle rider was perfectly willing to not control any other motorcycle on the track save his own. He did not worry about these other motorcycles since they had never injured him and the motorcycle racing game was still a game to him. However, during the accident there was a moment when he sought to control another motorcycle than his own and another rider. He failed in that effort. Thus in his *reactive mind* there is an actual mental image picture of his failing to control a motorcycle. Thus in future racing he is less competent. He is afraid of his own machine. He has identified his own machine with somebody else's machine. This is a failure of control.

---

13. **restimulated:** having a past memory reactivated due to similar circumstances in the present approximating circumstances of the past.

Now, in order to become a good motorcycle racer again this man would have to resume his attitude of carelessness regarding the control of the other machines and riders on the track and reassume his own ability to control his own machine. If he were able to do this, he would become once more a daring, efficient and winning motorcycle rider demonstrating great competence. Only a Scientology practitioner could put him back into this condition—and a Scientology practitioner would be able to do this probably in a very few hours. This, however, is not a textbook on how to eradicate former ills, but an explanation of why men become incompetent in the handling of their immediate tools of trade. These men have attempted to leave uncontrolled all the world around them up to the moment when the world around them hurt them. They then conceived the idea that they should control more than their own jobs. They failed to control more than their own jobs and were instantly convinced that they were incapable of controlling something. This is quite different than leaving things uncontrolled. To be capable of controlling things and to be capable of leaving things uncontrolled are both necessary to a good life and doing a good job. To become convinced that one cannot control something is an entirely different thing.

The whole feeling of self-confidence and competence actually derives from one's ability to control or leave uncontrolled the various items and people in his surroundings. When he becomes obsessed with a necessity to control something rather beyond his sphere of control, he is disabused[14] of his ability to control those things close to him. A person eventually gets into a state of mind where he cannot pay any attention at all to his own job but can only reach out into the outer environment and seek, effectively or otherwise, to stop, start or change things which have in

---

14. **disabused:** disillusioned; having had one's ideals taken away; made disappointed.

reality very little to do with his own job. Here we have the agitator, the inefficient worker, the individual who is going to fail. He is going to fail because he has failed at some time in the past.

This is not quite as hopeless as it looks because it takes actual physical injury and very heavy duress to make an individual feel that he is incapable of controlling things. The day-to-day handling of machinery is not what deteriorates one's ability to work or handle life. It is not true that one gets old and tired and his ability to do things wears out. It is true that one becomes injured in sudden, short moments and thereafter carries that injury into his future work and the injury is what causes him to deteriorate. The eradication of the injury brings him back to an ability to control his own environment.

The entire subject of work, then, brings us to the value of uncontrol. A machinist doing a good job should be able to relax as far as his machine is concerned. He should be able to let it run or not let it run, to start it or not to start it, to stop it or not to stop it. If he can do these things, all with confidence and a calm state of mind, he can then handle that machine and it will be discovered that the machine will run well for him.

Now let us say the machine bites him, he hurts his hand in it, some other worker jostles against him at the wrong moment, some tool given to him is defective and shatters. An actual physical pain enters into the situation. He tends to fall away from the machine. He tends then to concentrate much more heavily on the machine than he should. He is no longer willing to leave it uncontrolled. When he is working with that machine he *must control it*. Now, as he has entered duress into this situation and as he is already anxious about it, it is fairly certain that the machine will hurt him again. This gives him a second injury and with this injury he feels an even stronger urge to control the machine. You see, during the moments of injury the machine was out of control. Now while out-of-control is a game condition, it is not desired or welcome to this particular machinist. Eventually, it is certain he will look upon this machine as some sort of a demon. He will, you might say, run the machine all day and at night while asleep run it, too. He will spend his weekends and his holidays still running that machine. Eventually he will not be able to stand the sight of that machine and will flinch at the idea of working it a moment longer.

This picture becomes slightly complicated by the fact that it is not always the injury delivered to him by his own particular machine which causes him to feel anxious about machinery. A man who has been in an automobile accident may return to the working of a machine with considerable qualms[15] about machines in general. He begins to identify his own machine with other machines and all machines become the same machine and that is the machine that hurt him.

There are other conditions which enter into lighter phases of work. In the matter of a clerk, we may have a circumstance where he is ill from some other area than his area of work and yet, because he has little time off, is forced to work, sick or not. The tools of his own work, his filing cabinets or his pens or books or the very room, become identified with his feeling of sickness and he feels that these, too, have bitten him. Thus he becomes obsessed in his control of them and actually degenerates in his ability to control them just as the machinist does. Even though these tools have not actually injured him he associates them with being injured. In other words, he identifies his own sickness with the work he is doing. Thus even a clerk whose tools of trade are not particularly dangerous can become upset about his tools of trade and can first exert enormous control over

---

15. **qualms:** sudden feelings of uneasiness or doubt; misgivings.

them on an obsessed basis and at length abandon any control of them and feels he would rather be beaten than do an instant's more work in his particular sphere.

One of the ways of getting over such a condition is simply to touch or handle one's various tools of the trade and the surroundings in which he works. If a man were to go all the way around an office in which he had worked for years and touch the walls and window ledges and the equipment and tables and desks and chairs, ascertaining carefully the feel of each one, carefully locating each one with regard to the walls and other items in the room, he would feel much better about the entire room. He would be, in essence, moving himself from a moment of time where he was sick or injured, up to present time.[16] The maxim here is that one must do one's work in present time. One must not continue to work in old moments of injury.

If acquaintance with one's tools, or touching one's tools of the trade and discovering exactly where and how they are, is so beneficial, then what would be the mechanism behind this? We will leave until later in this book some drills and exercises calculated to rehabilitate one's ability to work, and look for a moment at this new factor.

---

16. **present time:** the time which is now and which becomes the past almost as rapidly as it is observed. It is a term loosely applied to the environment existing in now.

6

Affinity, Reality and Communication

6

Affinity, Reality and Communication

There are three factors in Scientology which are of the utmost importance in handling life. These three factors answer the questions: How should I talk to people? How can I sell people things? How can I give new ideas to people? How can I find what people are thinking about? How can I handle my work better?

We call these three factors in Scientology the ARC triangle. It is called a triangle because it has three related points. The first of these points is affinity. The second of these points is reality. The third of these points and the most important is communication.

These three factors are related. By affinity we mean emotional response. We mean the feeling of affection or lack of it, of emotion or misemotion[1] connected with life. By reality we mean the solid objects, the *real* things of life. By communication we mean an interchange of ideas between two terminals.[2] Without

---

1. **misemotion:** anything that is unpleasant emotion such as antagonism, anger, fear, grief, apathy or a death feeling.

2. **terminals:** anything used in a communication system; anything that can receive, relay or send a communication; a man would be a terminal, but a post (position, job or duty to which a person is assigned) would also be a terminal.

affinity there is no reality or communication. Without reality there is no affinity or communication. Without communication there is neither affinity nor reality. Now, these are sweeping statements but are nevertheless very valuable and are true.

Have you ever tried to talk to an angry man? An angry man's communication is at a level of misemotion which repels all terminals from him. Therefore his communication factor is very low, even though very loud. He is attempting to destroy something or some other terminal, therefore his reality is very poor. Very likely what he is being angry about apparently is not what has made him mad. An angry man is not truthful. Thus it could be said that his reality, even on the subject he is attempting to voice, is poor.

There must be good affinity (which is to say affection) between two people before they are very real to each other (and reality must here be used as a gradient, with some things being more real than other things). There must be good affinity between two people before they can talk together with any truth or confidence. Before two people can be real to each other there must be some communication between them. They must at least see each other, which is in itself a form of communication. Before two people can feel any affinity for each other they must, to some degree, be real.

These three terms are interdependent one upon the other, and when one drops the other two drop also. When one rises the other two rise also. It is only necessary to improve one corner of this very valuable triangle in Scientology in order to improve the remaining two corners. It is only necessary to improve two corners of the triangle to improve the third.

To give you some idea of a practical application of this, there is the case of a young girl who had run away from home and whose parents would no longer talk to her. The girl, as a clerk in an office, was quite despondent[3] and was doing very bad work. A Scientologist whose attention had been directed to her by the office manager gave her an interview and discovered that her parents were intensely angry with her and would no longer communicate with her at all. They had been so upset at her refusal (actually her inability) to follow a career as a concert pianist, for which they had her studying at great expense, that they had "washed their hands of her," and the unpleasantness had forced her to run away to a distant point. Since that time they had not communicated with her but had spoken to people she had known in her home neighborhood in very bitter terms concerning her.

In such a state of mind, since she was intimately involved with her parents and wished to be on the best possible terms with them, she could not work. Her failure to perform her work was jamming communication lines in her own office. In other words, her affinity was very low and her reality on things was quite low since she might be said to have been elsewhere most of the time, and thus the communication lines which passed through her hands were equally low and successfully jammed other communication lines in the office, at which time this matter became of intense interest to the office manager. Now, ordinarily in the workaday world the office manager would have dismissed her and found another girl. But employment was critical at the time and this office manager knew the modern thing to do. He sent for a Scientologist.

The Scientologist, knowing well this ARC triangle, did a very ordinary thing—to a Scientologist—which apparently worked magic as far as the girl was concerned. He told the girl that she must write to her parents—regardless of whether they

---

3. **despondent:** feeling or showing profound hopelessness or discouragement.

replied or not she must write—and she did so. Naturally there was no reply. Why was there no reply from the parents? Well, the girl, having disobeyed them and having moved out from underneath their control, was apparently no longer in contact with them. These parents did not consider her as real. She did not actually exist as far as they were concerned. They had actually said this to themselves. They had actually tried to wipe her out of their lives since she was such a disappointment. Therefore they had no emotion about her whatsoever except perhaps a sort of apathy. They had been unable to control her and so they were apathetic about her since they had failed to control her. At this stage the parents were glumly apathetic about the girl and she was not very real to them at all. As a matter of fact, as they had started her on a career she could not complete, the girl could not have been very real to them in the first place since the career was undoubtedly beyond the girl's capabilities. So the Scientologist had her write a letter. This letter was, as we say in Scientology, entirely "good roads and good weather." The girl said that she was working in this other city, that the weather was good, that she was getting along well, and hoped that they were both well and sent them her love. The letter carefully did not take up any of the problems or activities immediately behind her leaving home. The A of the letter, the affinity, was quite high; the C was present. What the Scientologist was trying to do was establish R, reality: the reality of the situation of the girl's being in another city and the actual reality of her existence in the world. He knew that she was sufficiently involved with her parents that if they did not consider her real, she was not even real to herself. Of course, the parents did not answer this first letter but the Scientologist had the girl write again.

After four letters, all of which said more or less the same things and entirely ignored the idea that there had been no reply, there was a sudden letter from the mother to the girl which was angry, not with the girl but with one of her old playmates. The girl, coached, was held in line by the Scientologist and was not permitted to explode back through the communication line but was coaxed into writing a surprised, pleasant letter expressing her happiness at having heard from her mother. After this two letters came, one from the father and one from the mother, both of them were very affectionate and hoped the girl was doing well. The girl of course replied to these very joyously but would have been completely propitiative[4] if the Scientologist had permitted her to do so. Instead, a happy letter went back to each of them, and in return two more letters came, both of them very congratulatory to the girl at having found a job and found something that she was interested in doing in life, with requests as to where her clothes should be sent and actually a small draft of money to help her along in the city. The parents had already begun to plan the new career of the girl which was in exact line with what the girl could do in life—stenographic work.

Of course, the Scientologist knew exactly what was going to happen. He knew that their affinity and reality would come up and the girl's reality, affinity and communication in the office itself would rise as soon as this situation was remedied. He remedied with communication, expressing affinity from the girl and this of course, as it always does, produced reaction. The girl's work came up to par, the girl began to progress and, now that her feeling of reality was sufficiently high, actually became a very valuable office worker.

Probably the reason why the ARC triangle went so long undiscovered was the fact that a person in apathy rises through various tones. These tones are quite uniform; one follows the next and people *always* come up through these tones one after

---

4. **propitiative:** acting in a manner calculated to reduce the anger or win the favor of another; trying to make calm or quiet.

the other. These are the tones of affinity, and the Tone Scale[5] of Dianetics[6] and Scientology is probably the best possible way of predicting what is going to happen next or what a person actually will do.

The Tone Scale starts well below apathy. In other words, a person is feeling no emotion about a subject at all. An example of this was the American attitude concerning the atomic bomb; something about which they should have been very concerned was so far beyond their ability to control and so likely to end their existence that they were below apathy about it. They actually did not even feel that it was very much of a problem. Americans processed on this particular subject had to be worked with for some little time until they began to feel apathetic about the atomic bomb. This was really an advance over the feeling of no emotion whatsoever on a subject which should have intimately concerned them. In other words, on many subjects and problems people are actually well below apathy. There the Tone Scale starts, on utter, dead null far below death itself. Going up into improved tones one encounters the level of body death, apathy, grief, fear, anger, antagonism, boredom, enthusiasm and serenity, in that order. There are many small stops between these tones, but one knowing anything about human beings should definitely know these particular emotions. A person who is in apathy, when his tone is improved, feels grief. A person in grief, when his tone improves, feels fear. A person in fear, when his tone improves, feels anger. A person in anger, when his tone

---

5. **Tone Scale:** the scale of emotional states which range from death at the bottom, up through apathy, grief, fear, covert hostility, anger, antagonism, boredom, conservatism, cheerfulness to enthusiasm at the top. (Actually higher and lower tone levels exist than those named.)

6. **Dianetics:** man's most advanced school of the mind. The word comes from Greek *dia,* "through," and *nous,* "soul." Dianetics is defined as what the soul is doing to the body. It is a way of handling the energy of which life is made in such a way as to bring about a greater efficiency in the organism and in the spiritual life of the individual.

improves, feels antagonism. A person in antagonism, when his tone improves, feels boredom. When a person in boredom improves his tone, he is enthusiastic. When an enthusiastic person improves his tone, he feels serenity. Actually the below apathy level is so low as to constitute a no-affinity, no-emotion, no-problem, no-consequence state of mind on things which are actually tremendously important.

The area below apathy is an area without pain, interest, beingness[7] or anything else that matters to anyone, but it is an area of grave danger since one is below the level of being able to respond to anything and may accordingly lose everything without apparently noticing it. A workman who is in very bad condition and who is actually a liability to the organization may not be capable of experiencing pain or any emotion on any subject. He is below apathy. We have seen workmen who would hurt their hand and think nothing of it and go right on working even though their hand was very badly injured. People in dispensaries[8] working in industrial areas are quite amazed sometimes to discover how little attention some workmen pay to their own injuries. It is an ugly fact that people who pay no attention to their own injuries and who are not even feeling pain from those injuries are not and never will be, without some attention from a Scientologist, efficient people. They are liabilities to have around. They do not respond properly. If such a person is working a crane and the crane suddenly goes out of control to dump its load on a group of men, that subapathy crane operator will simply let the crane drop its load. In other words, he is a potential murderer. He cannot stop anything, he cannot change

---

7. **beingness:** the assumption or choosing of a category of identity. Beingness is assumed by oneself or given to oneself or is attained. Examples of beingness would be one's own name, one's profession, one's physical characteristics, one's role in a game—each and all of these things could be called one's beingness.

8. **dispensaries:** rooms or places, as in schools, camps or factories, where medicines and first-aid treatment are available.

anything and he cannot start anything and yet, on some automatic response basis, he manages some of the time to hold down a job, but the moment a real emergency confronts him he is not likely to respond properly and accidents result. Where there are accidents in industry they stem from these people in the subapathy tone range. Where bad mistakes are made in offices which cost firms a great deal of money, lost time and cause other personnel difficulties, such mistakes are found rather uniformly to stem from these subapathy people. So do not think that one of these states of being unable to feel anything, of being numb, of being incapable of pain or joy is any use to anyone. It is not. A person who is in this condition cannot control things and in actuality is not *there* sufficiently to be controlled by anyone else and does strange and unpredictable things.

Just as a person can be chronically in subapathy, so a person can be in apathy. This is dangerous enough but is at least expressed. Only when we get up into apathy itself do we have the ARC triangle beginning to manifest itself and become visible. Communication from the person himself, not from some circuit[9] or training pattern[10] is to be expected. People can be chronically in grief, chronically in fear, chronically in anger, or in antagonism, or boredom, or actually can be "stuck in enthusiasm." A person who is truly able is normally fairly serene about things. He can, however, express other emotions. It is a mistake to believe that a total serenity is of any real value. When a situation which demands tears cannot be cried about, one is not in serenity as a chronic tone. Serenity can be mistaken rather easily for subapathy, but of course only by a very untrained observer. One glance at the physical condition of the person is enough to

9. **circuit:** a part of an individual's mind that behaves as though it were someone or something separate from him and either dictates or takes over his actions.

10. **training pattern:** a stimulus-response mechanism set up by the analytical mind to carry out activity of either a routine or an emergency nature.

differentiate. People who are in subapathy are normally quite ill.

Just as we have a range of the Tone Scale thus covering the subject of affinity, so do we have one for communication. On the level of each of the emotions we have a communication factor. In subapathy an individual is not really communicating at all. Some social response or training pattern or, as we say, "circuit" is communicating. The person himself does not seem to be there and isn't really talking. Therefore his communications are sometimes strange to say the least. He does the wrong things at the wrong time. He says the wrong things at the wrong time. Naturally when a person is stuck on any of the bands of the Tone Scale—subapathy, apathy, grief, fear, anger, antagonism, boredom, enthusiasm or serenity—he voices communications with that emotional tone. A person who is always angry about something is stuck in anger. Such a person is not as bad off as somebody in subapathy, but he is still rather dangerous to have around since he will make trouble, and a person who is angry does not control things well. The communication characteristics of people at these various levels on the Tone Scale are quite fascinating. They say things and handle communication each in a distinct characteristic fashion for each level of the Tone Scale.

Just as in affinity and communication, there is a level of reality for each of the affinity levels. Reality is an intensely interesting subject since it has to do, in the main, with relative solids. In other words, the solidity of things and the emotional tone of people have a definite connection. People low on the Tone Scale cannot tolerate solids. They cannot tolerate a solid object. The thing is not real to them; it is thin or lacking weight. As they come upscale, the same object becomes more and more solid and they can finally see it in its true level of solidity. In other words, these people have a definite reaction to mass at various points on the scale. Things are bright to them or very, very dull. If you could look through the eyes of the person in subapathy you would see a very watery, thin, dreamy, misty, unreal world indeed. If you looked through the eyes of an angry man you would see a world which was menacingly solid, where all the solids posed a brutality toward him, but they still would not be sufficiently solid or sufficiently real or visible for a person in good condition. A person in serenity can see solids as they are, as bright as they are, and can tolerate an enormous heaviness or solidity without reacting to it. In other words, as we go up the Tone Scale from the lowest to the highest, things can get more and more solid and more and more real.

Affinity is most closely related to space. In fact affinity could be defined as the "consideration of distance" since terminals which are far apart or close together have different affinity reactions one to another. Reality, as we have seen, is most intimately connected with solids. Communication consists of the flow of ideas or particles across space between solids.

While these definitions may seem very elementary and would not at all satisfy an M.I.T.[11] professor, they actually outreach and encompass an M.I.T. professor's whole field of activity. Truths do not have to be complicated.

There are, as described at considerable length and studied with considerable depth in Scientology, many interrelations of spaces and solids, and ideas or particles, since these are the most intimate things to livingness itself and comprise the universe around us. But the most basic thing we should know about ARC is simply emotional tone which is affinity, the actuality of things which is reality, and the relative communication ability concerning them.

---

11. **M.I.T.:** Massachusetts Institute of Technology, a university in Massachusetts specializing in the teaching of science and technology.

Men who can do things are very high on affinity, very high in terms of reality and are very capable in terms of communication. If you wish to measure their various capabilities you should study the subject much further. A whole book has been written about this triangle called *Science of Survival.* [See Bibliography.]

Then how would you talk to a man? You cannot talk adequately to a man if you are in a subapathy condition. In fact, you would not talk to him at all. You would have to have a little higher affinity than that to discuss things with anyone. Your ability to talk to any given man has to do with your emotional response to any given man. Anyone has different emotional responses to different people around him. In view of the fact that two terminals, or, that is to say, two people, are always involved in communication, one could see that someone else would have to be somewhat real. If one does not care about other people at all, one will have a great deal of difficulty talking to them, that is certain. The way to talk to a man, then, would be to find something to like about him and to discuss something with which he can agree. This is the downfall of most new ideas: One does not discuss subjects with which the other person has any point of agreement at all. And we come to a final factor with regard to reality.

That with which we agree tends to be more real than that with which we do not agree. There is a definite coordination between agreement and reality. Those things are real which we agree are real. Those things are not real which we agree are not real. On those things upon which we disagree we have very little reality. An experiment based on this would be an even jocular discussion between two men of a third man who is present. The two men agree on something with which the third man cannot agree. The third man will drop in emotional tone and will actually become less real to the two people who are discussing him.

How do you talk to a man then? You establish reality by finding something with which you both agree. Then you attempt to maintain as high an affinity level as possible by knowing there is something you can like about him. And you are then able to talk with him. If you do not have the first two conditions, it is fairly certain that the third condition will not be present, which is to say, you will not be able to talk to him easily.

You should realize in using the ARC triangle that, once more, the emotional tones are progressed through as one begins to develop communication. In other words, somewhere up the line somebody who has been totally apathetic about us is liable to become angry at us. If one can simply persevere up through this anger, he reaches only antagonism, then boredom and finally enthusiasm and a perfect communication level and under-standing. Marriages fall apart simply because of a failure of communication, because of a failure of reality and affinity. When communication starts failing the affinity starts dropping. People have secrets from each other and the affinity starts out the bottom.

Similarly, in an office or a business, it is perfectly easy to establish those people who are doing things which are not to the best interests of the firm, since these people go gradually and sometimes not so gradually out of communication with the firm. Their emotional tone toward their superiors and those around them starts dropping and finally goes out the bottom.

As can be seen, the ARC triangle is intimately bound up with an ability to control and an ability to leave uncontrolled. When an individual attempts to control something and fails to do so he then experiences an antipathy[12] toward that thing. In other words, he has not been right, he has been wrong. His

---

12. **antipathy:** a strong or deep-rooted dislike.

---

intention has failed. His intention has, you might say, backfired upon him. Thus as one attempts to control things and then fails to control them he is likely to drop down Tone Scale about those things. Thus an individual who has been betrayed by the tools of his own trade is apt to treat them with a lowering affinity level. He becomes bored with them, he becomes antagonistic toward them, he becomes angry with them—and at this stage the machinery starts to break up—and finally he becomes afraid of them, becomes sad about them, becomes apathetic about them and no longer cares about them at all, and at this stage certainly cannot use them at all. Actually from the level of boredom down the ability to use one's tools of the trade is consistently lowered.

Now, how could one knowing this raise his ability to control the tools of the trade without even going to a Scientologist? Naturally, if a Scientologist took over in this situation the entirety of control of tools or an area or of life could be regained, but, lacking this, how could one simply handle the exact articles with which he is right now and immediately associated?

By using ARC he could regain in some measure both his control of the tools and his enthusiasm for work. He would do this by communicating and discovering his willingness for these and the people around him to be real or solid. An individual could regain his ability over his immediate tools simply by touching them and letting them go. This might seem rather pointless and he is apt to reach the level of boredom and become bored with the process. Just above this level is the pay of becoming enthusiastic. It sounds very strange that if one simply touched his automobile and let go and touched it and let go and touched it and let go and touched it and let go, possibly for some hours, he would regain not only his enthusiasm for the automobile but a tremendous ability to control the car which he had never suspected in himself at all. Similarly with people, since these often object to being touched, one can communicate. If one really communicates and communicates well to these people, listens to what they have to say and acknowledges what they say and says what he has to say to them gently enough and often enough so that it is actually received by them, he will regain to a very marked degree his ability to associate and coordinate the actions of those people with whom he is immediately surrounded. Here we have ARC immediately adjusted to work. It sounds strange that if we made a bookkeeper pick up and lay down his pencil or pen for a couple of hours he would regain his ability to handle it and would improve in his ability to make figures; and that if we got him to touch and let go of his ledger for a considerable length of time he would be more capable of handling that ledger and would make far fewer mistakes with it. This sounds like magic. It is magic. It is Scientology.

7

Exhaustion

7

Exhaustion

To work or not to work, that is the question. The answer to that question in most men's minds is exhaustion.

One begins to feel, after he has been long on a job and has been considerably abused on that job, that to work any more would be quite beyond his endurance. He is tired. The thought of doing certain things makes him tired. He thinks of raising his energy or of being able to force his way along just a little bit further, and if he does so he is thinking in the wrong channels since the answer to exhaustion has little if anything to do with energy.

Exhaustion is a very important subject, not only to an individual involved in earning his own living but to the state as well.

Scientology has rather completely established the fact that the downfall of the individual begins when he is no longer able to work. All it is necessary to do to degrade or upset an individual is to prevent him from working. Even the police have now come to recognize the basic Scientology principle that the primary thing wrong with a criminal is that he cannot work, and police have begun to look for this factor in an individual in establishing his criminality.

The basic difficulty with all juvenile delinquency is the one-time apparently humane program of forbidding children to labor in any way. Doubtless it was once a fact that child labor was abused, that children were worked too hard, that their growths were stunted[1] and that they were, in general, used. It is highly doubtful if the infamous Mr. Marx[2] ever saw in America young boys being pulled off machines dead from work and thrown onto dump heaps. Where there was an abuse of this matter, there was a public outcry against it, and legislation was enacted to prevent children from working. This legislation with all the good intention of the world is, however, directly responsible for juvenile delinquency. Forbidding children to work, and particularly forbidding teenagers to make their own way in the world and earn their own money, creates a family difficulty so that it becomes almost impossible to raise a family, and creates as well, and particularly, a state of mind in the teenager that the world does not want him, and he has already lost his game before he has begun it. Then with something like universal military training staring him in the face so that he dare not start a career, he is of course thrust into a deep subapathy on the subject of work, and when he at length is faced with the necessity of making his own way in the world, he rises into an apathy and does nothing about it at all. It is highly supportive of this fact that our greatest citizens worked, usually when they were quite young. In the Anglo-American[3] civilization the highest level of endeavor was achieved by boys who, from the age of twelve, on farms, had their own duties and had a definite place in the world.

Children, in the main, are quite willing to work. A two-,

---

1. **stunted:** stopped or slowed down, hindered.

2. **Marx, Karl:** (1818–83) German political philosopher. Regarded by some as the founder of modern socialism.

3. **Anglo-American:** belonging to, relating to or involving England and America, especially the United States, or the people of the two countries.

three-, four-year-old child is usually found haunting his father or her mother trying to help out either with tools or dust rags; and the kind parent who is really fond of the children responds in the reasonable and long-ago-normal manner of being patient enough to let the child actually assist. A child so permitted then develops the idea that his presence and activity is desired and he quite calmly sets about a career of accomplishment. The child who is warped or pressed into some career, but is not permitted to assist in those early years, is convinced that he is not wanted, that the world has no part of him. And later on he will come into very definite difficulties regarding work. However, the child who at three or four wants to work in this modern society is discouraged and is actually prevented from working, and after he is made to be idle until seven, eight or nine, is suddenly saddled with certain chores. Now this child is already educated into the fact that he must not work and so the idea of work is a sphere where he "knows he does not belong," and so he always feels uncomfortable in performing various activities. Later on in his teens, he is actively prevented from getting the sort of a job which will permit him to buy the clothes and treats for his friends which he feels are demanded of him, and so he begins to feel he is not a part of the society. Not being part of the society, he is then against the society and desires nothing but destructive activities.

The subject of exhaustion is also the subject of prevented work. In the case of soldiers and sailors hospitalized during any one of these recent wars, it is found that a few months in the hospital tends to break the morale of the soldier or sailor to such a point that he may become a questionable asset when returned to his service. This is not necessarily the result of his lowered abilities. It is the result of injury compounded by inactivity. A soldier who is wounded and cared for in a field hospital close to the front and is returned to duty the moment he can possibly support such duties will be found to retain, in a large measure, his morale. Of course the injury received has a tendency to repel him from the level of action which he once thought best but, even so, he is in better shape than a soldier who is sent to a hospital in the rear. The soldier who is sent to the hospital in the rear is being told, according to his viewpoint, that he is not particularly necessary to the war. Without actually adding up these principles, the word *exhaustion* began a general use coupled with neurosis. This was based on the fact that people with a neurosis simply looked exhausted. There was no more coordination to it than that. Actually, a person who has been denied the right to work, particularly one who has been injured and then denied the right to work, will eventually encounter exhaustion.

Technically in Scientology it is discovered that there is no such thing as gradual diminishing by continuing contact of the energy of the individual. One does not become exhausted simply because one has worked too long or too hard. One becomes exhausted when he has worked sufficiently long to restimulate some old injury. One of the characteristics of this injury will be exhaustion. Chronic exhaustion, then, is not the product of long hours and arduous application. It is the product of the accumulation of the shocks and injuries incident[4] to life, each of them perhaps only a few seconds or a few hours long and adding up perhaps to a totality of only fifty or seventy-five hours. But this accumulation—the accumulation of injury, repulsion and shock —eventually mounts up to a complete inability to do anything.

Exhaustion can then be trained into a person by refusing to allow him as a child to have any part in the society, or it can be beaten into a person by the various injuries or shocks he may receive incident to his particular activities. Clear up either of these two points and you have cleared up exhaustion. Exhaustion, then, is actually the subject of a Scientology practitioner

---

4. **incident:** liable to happen, accompanying something.

since only a Scientologist can adequately handle it.

There is a point, however, which is below exhaustion. This is the point of not knowing when one is tired. An individual can become a sort of hectic puppet that goes on working and working without even realizing that he is working at all, and suddenly collapses from a tiredness he was not experiencing. This is our subzero or subapathy Tone Scale again.

And again we have the subject of control. Here the individual has failed to control things, has tried and then gone down Tone Scale about them into the subzero band. Eventually he is incapable of handling anything even resembling tools of the trade or an environment of work and so is unable to inhabit such an environment or handle such tools. The individual can then have many hard words cast in his direction. He can be called lazy, he can be called a bum, he can be called criminal. But the truth of the matter is he is no more capable of righting his own condition without expert help than he is capable of diving to the center of the Earth.

There are some means of recovering one's verve[5] and enthusiasm for work short of close[6] work with a Scientology practitioner. These are relatively simple and very easy to understand.

We have in Scientology something we call introversion and something else we call extroversion.

Introversion is a simple thing. It means looking in too closely. And extroversion is also a simple thing. It means nothing more than being able to look outward.

---

5. **verve:** vigor and energy, as in movement, etc.

6. **close:** thorough; careful.

It could be said that there are introverted personalities and extroverted personalities. An extroverted personality is one who is capable of looking around the environment. An introverted personality is only capable of looking inward at himself.

When we examine the ARC Tone Scale we see at once that an introverted personality is shying away from solids. In other words, he is not confronting reality. Reality is agreement in the mental plane[7] and is solids in the physical plane.

A person who is capable of looking at the world around him and seeing it quite real and quite bright is, of course, in a state of extroversion. He can look out, in other words. He can also work. He can also see situations and handle and control those things which he has to handle and control, and can stand by and watch those things which he does not have to control and be interested in them therefore.

The person who is introverted is a person who has probably passed exhaustion some way back. He has had his attention focused closer and closer to him (basically by old injuries which are still capable of exerting their influence upon him) until he is actually looking inward and not outward. He is shying away from solid objects. He does not see a reality in other people and things around him.

Now let us take the actual subject of work. Work is the application of attention and action to people or objects located in space.

When one is no longer able to confront people or objects or the space in which they are located, he begins to have a lost feeling. He begins to move in a mistiness. Things are not real to

---

7. **plane:** a level of development, achievement, existence, etc.

---

him and he is relatively incapable of controlling those things around him. He has accidents. He has bad luck. He has things turn against him simply because he is not handling them or controlling them or even observing them correctly. The future to him seems very bad, so bad sometimes that he cannot face it. This person could be said to be severely introverted.

In work his attention is riveted on objects which are usually at the most only a few feet from him. He pays his closest attention to articles which are within the reach of his hands. This puts his attention away from extroversion at least to some spot in focus in front of his face. His attention fixes there. If this is co-incident with some old injury incident or operation, he is likely to fix his attention as well on some spot in former times and become restimulated, so that he gets the pains and ills and the feeling of tiredness or apathy or subapathy which he had during that moment of injury. As his attention is continuously riveted there he of course has a tendency to look only there, even when he is not working.

Let us take an accountant. An accountant's eyes are on books at fixed distances from his eyes. At length he becomes "shortsighted."[8] Actually he doesn't become shortsighted, he becomes book-sighted. His eyes most easily fix on a certain point in distance. Now as he fixes his attention there he tends to withdraw even from that point until at length he does not quite reach even his own books. Then he is fitted with glasses so that he can see the books more clearly. His vision and his attention are much the same thing.

A person who has a machine or books or objects continually at a fixed distance from him leaves his work and tends to keep his attention fixed exactly where his work was. In other words,

---

8. **shortsighted:** able to see clearly only what is close.

his attention never really leaves his work at all. Although he goes home he is still really sitting in the office. His attention is still fixed on the environment of his work. If this environment is coincident with some injury or accident (and who does not have one of these at least?), he begins to feel weariness or tiredness.

Is there a cure for this?

Of course, only a Scientology practitioner could clear up this difficulty entirely. But the worker does have something which he can do.

Now here is the wrong thing to do, regardless of whether one is a bookkeeper, an accountant, a clerk, an executive or a machinist. The wrong thing to do is to leave work, go home, sit down and fix attention on an object more or less at the same distance from one as one confronts continually at work. In the case of a foreman, for instance, who is continually talking to men at a certain distance away from him, the wrong thing for him to do is to go home and talk to his wife at the same distance. The next thing she knows, she will be getting orders just as though she were a member of the shop. Definitely the wrong thing to do is to go home and sit down and read a paper, eat some dinner and go to bed. If a man practiced the routine of working all day and then sitting down "to rest" with a book or a newspaper in the evening, it is certain that sooner or later he would start to feel quite exhausted and then after a while would fall even below that and would not even wonder at his unwillingness to perform tasks which were once very easy to him.

Is there a right thing to do? Yes, there is. An individual who is continually fixed upon some object of work should fix his attention otherwise after working hours.

Now here is a process known as "Take a Walk." This process is very easy to perform. When one feels tired on finishing his work, no matter if the thought of doing so is almost all that he can tolerate without falling through the floor, he should go out and walk around the block until he feels rested. In short, he should walk around the block and look at things until he sees the things he is walking near. It does not matter how many times he walked around the block, he should walk around the block until he feels better.

In doing this it will be found that one will become a little brighter at first and then will become very much more tired. He will become sufficiently tired that he knows now that he should go to bed and have a good night's sleep. This is not the time to stop walking since he is walking through exhaustion. He is walking out his exhaustion. He is not handling the exhaustion by physical exercise. The physical exercise has always appeared to be the more important factor to people, but the exercise is relatively unimportant. The factor that is important is the unfixing of his attention from his work to the material world in which he is living.

Masses are reality. To increase one's affinity and communication it is actually necessary to be able to confront and tolerate masses. Therefore walking around the block and looking at buildings will be found to bring one upscale. When one is so tired that he can barely drag himself around, or is so tired that he is hectically unable to rest at all, it is actually necessary that he confront masses. He is simply low on the Tone Scale. It is even doubtful if there is such a thing as a "fall of physical energy." Naturally there is a limit to this process. One cannot work all day and walk around the block all night and go to work the next day again and still expect to feel relieved. But one should certainly spend some time extroverting after having introverted all day.

"Take a Walk" is, within reason, a near cure-all. If one feels antagonistic toward one's wife, the wrong thing to do is to beat her. The right thing to do is to go out and take a walk around the block until one feels better, and make her walk around the block in the opposite direction until an extroversion from the situation is achieved. It will be discovered that all domestic quarrels, particularly amongst working people, stem from the fact that, having been overfixed[9] (rather than overstrained) on one's work and the situations connected with it, one has failed to control certain things in his working environment. He then comes home and seeks to find something he *can* control. This is usually the marital partner or the children, and when one fails even there he is apt to drop downscale with a vengeance.

The extroversion of attention is as necessary as the work itself. There is nothing really wrong with introverting attention or with work. If one didn't have something to be interested in, he would go to pieces entirely. But if one works, it will be found that an unnatural tiredness is apt to set in. When this is found to be the case then the answer to this is not a drop into unconsciousness for a few hours, as in sleep, but in actually extroverting the attention and then getting a really relaxing sleep.

These principles of extroversion and introversion have many ramifications[10] and, although "Take a Walk" is almost laughable in its simplicity, there are many more complicated processes in case one wished to get more complicated. However, in the main, "Take a Walk" will take care of an enormous number of difficulties attendant to work. Remember that when doing it one will get more tired at first and will then get fresher. This phenomenon has been noted by athletes. It is called the second wind. The second wind is really getting enough environment and enough mass in order to run out the exhaustion of the last race. There is

9. **overfixed:** too set or intent upon something; steadily directed to an excessive degree.

10. **ramifications:** derived effects, consequences or results.

no such thing as a second wind. There *is* such a thing as a return to extroversion on the physical world in which one lives.

Similar to "Take a Walk" is another process known as "Look Them Over." If one has been talking to people all day, has been selling people all day or has been handling people who are difficult to handle all day, the wrong thing to do is to run away from all the people there are in the world. You see, the person who gets overstrained when handling people has had large difficulties with people. He has perhaps been operated upon by doctors, and the half-seen vision of them standing around the operating table identifies all people with doctors; that is to say, all people who stand still. This, by the way, is one of the reasons why doctors become so thoroughly hated in a society since they do insist on practices known as surgery and anesthesia and such incidents become interlocked with everyday incidents.

Exhaustion because of contact with people actually necessitates that the "havingness"[11] (another Scientology term for reality) of people has been reduced. One's attention has been fixated upon certain people while his attention, he felt, ought to be on other people, and this straining of attention has actually cut down the number of people that he was observing. Fixed attention, then, upon a few people can actually limit the number of people one can "have," which is to say, limits one's reality on people in general.

The cure for this is a very simple one. One should go to a place that is very well populated such as a railroad station or a main street and should simply walk along the street noting people. Simply look at people—that is all. It will be found after a

---

11. **havingness:** the concept of being able to reach. By havingness we mean owning, possessing, being capable of commanding, taking charge of objects, energies and spaces.

while that one feels people aren't so bad and one has a much kinder attitude toward them and, more importantly, the job condition of becoming overstrained with people tends to go away if one makes a practice of doing this every late afternoon for a few weeks.

This is one of the smartest things that a salesman can do, since a salesman, above and beyond others, has a vested interest in being able to handle people and get them to do exactly what he wants them to do, that is, buy what he has to sell. As he fixes his attention on just one too many customers, he gets tired of the whole idea of talking to people or selling and goes down Tone Scale in all of his activities and operations and begins to consider himself all kinds of a swindler and at length doesn't consider himself anything at all. He, like the others, should simply find populated places and walk along looking at people. He will find after a while that people really do exist and that they aren't so bad. One of the things that happens to people in high government is that they are being continually "protected from" the people and they at length become quite disgusted with the whole subject and are apt to do all manner of strange things. (See the lives of Hitler[12] and Napoleon.)

This principle of extroversion and introversion could go much further in a society than it does. There is something that could be done by the government and by businesses in general which would probably eradicate the idea of strikes and would increase production quite markedly. Workers who strike are usually discontented, not so much with the conditions of work, but with work itself. They feel they are being victimized, they are being pressed into working at times when they do not want to

---

12. **Hitler, Adolf:** (1889–1945) dictator of Germany from 1933 to 1945. In rising to power in Germany, he fortified his position through murder of real or imagined opponents and maintained police-state control over the population. He lead Germany into World War II resulting in its nearly total destruction.

work, and a strike comes as an actual relief. They can fight something. They can do something else than stand there and fiddle with a piece of machinery or account books. Dissatisfied workers are striking workers. If people become exhausted at work, if people are not content with work, if people are upset with work, they can be counted upon to find a sufficient number of grievances to strike. And, if management is given enough trouble and lack of cooperation on the part of the people on the lower chains of command, it can be certain that management sooner or later will create situations which cause workers to strike. In other words, bad conditions of work are actually not the reason for labor troubles and disputes. Weariness of work itself or an inability to control the area and environments of work *are* the actual cause of labor difficulties.

Any management given sufficient income to do so, if that management is not terribly aberrated, will pay a decent working wage. And any workman given half a chance will perform his duties cheerfully. But once the environment itself becomes over-strained, once the company itself has become introverted by overt acts[13] on the part of the government, once the workers have been shown that they have no control over management, there can be, after that, labor disputes. Underlying all these obvious principles, however, are the principles of introversion and extro-version. Workers become so introverted at their tasks that they no longer are capable of affinity for their leaders and are no longer capable actually of viewing the environment in which they work. Therefore someone can come along and tell them that all the executives are ogres, which is obviously not true, and on the executive level someone can come along and tell the executives that all the workers are ogres, which is obviously, on that side, not true either.

---

13. **overt acts:** intentionally committed harmful acts committed in an effort to resolve a problem.

In the absence of broad treatment on individuals, which is a gargantuan[14] task, a full program could be worked out that would handle the principle of introversion. It is certain that if workers or managers get introverted enough they will then find ways and means of inventing aberrated games such as strikes, and so disrupt production and decent relationships and living conditions within the factory, the office, or the concern.

The cure would be to extrovert workers on a very broad scale. This could be done, as one solution, by making it possible for all workers to have two jobs. It would be necessary for the company, or related interests such as the government, to make available a sufficient number of public works projects to provide work for workers outside the sphere of exact application. In other words, a man who is made to work continually inside and at a very fixed task would find a considerable relief at being able to go outside and work, particularly at some disrelated task. As an example, it would be a considerable relief to an accountant to be able to dig ditches for a while. A machinist running a stationary machine would actually find it a very joyful experience to push around a bulldozer.

Such a plan then would actually take introversion and extroversion with a large hand and bring it about. Workers who are working in fixed positions with their attention very close to them would then be permitted to look more widely and to handle things which tended to extrovert them. Such a program would be very ambitious but it would be found, it is certain, to result in better labor-management relations, better production and a considerable lessening of working and public tension on the subjects of jobs and pay.

In short, there are many things that could be done with the

---

14. **gargantuan:** gigantic, enormous, colossal.

basic principle of extroversion–introversion. The principle is very simple: When an individual is made too introverted, things become less real in his surroundings and he has less affinity for them and cannot communicate with them well. Furthermore, what does communicate is apt to communicate at his lowered Tone Scale so that even good news will be poorly received by him. In such a condition he becomes tired easily. Introversion results in weariness, exhaustion and then an inability to work. The remedy for it is extroversion, a good look at and communication with the wider environment, and unless this is practiced, then, in view of the fact that any worker is subject to injuries or illnesses of one kind or another, a dwindling spiral will ensue which makes work less and less palatable[15] until at length it cannot be performed at all, and we have the basis of not only a nonproductive, but a criminal society.

---

15. **palatable:** acceptable to the mind.

8

The Man
Who Succeeds

8

The Man
Who Succeeds

The conditions of success are few and easily stated.

Jobs are not held consistently and in actuality by flukes[1] of fate or fortune. Those who depend upon luck generally experience bad luck. The ability to hold a job depends, in the main, upon ability. One must be able to control his work and must be able to be controlled in doing his work. One must be able, as well, to leave certain areas uncontrolled. One's intelligence is directly related to his ability. There is no such thing as being too smart. But there is such a thing as being too stupid.

But one may be both able and intelligent without succeeding. A vital part of success is the ability to handle and control, not only one's tools of the trade, but the people with whom one is surrounded. In order to do this one must be capable of a very high level of affinity, he must be able to tolerate massive realities and he must also be able to give and receive communication.

The ingredients of success are then: first, an ability to confront work with joy and not horror; a wish to do work for its own sake, not because one "has to have a paycheck." One must

---

1. **flukes:** accidental strokes of good luck.

be able to work without driving oneself or experiencing deep depths of exhaustion. If one experiences these things there is something wrong with him. There is some element in his environment that he should be controlling that he isn't controlling, or his accumulated injuries are such as to make him shy away from all people and masses with whom he should be in intimate contact.

The ingredients of successful work are: training and experience in the subject being addressed, good general intelligence and ability, a capability of high affinity, a tolerance of reality, and the ability to communicate and receive ideas. Given these things there is left only a slim chance of failure. Given these things a man can ignore all of the accidents of birth, marriage or fortune; for birth, marriage and fortune are not capable of placing these necessary ingredients in one's hands. One could have all the money in the world and yet be unable to perform an hour's honest labor. Such a man would be a miserably unhappy one.

The person who studiously[2] avoids work usually works far longer and far harder than the man who pleasantly confronts it and does it. Men who cannot work are not happy men.

Work is the stable datum of this society. Without something to do there is nothing for which to live. A man who cannot work is as good as dead and usually prefers death and works to achieve it.

The mysteries of life are not today, with Scientology, very mysterious. Mystery is not a needful ingredient. Only the very aberrated man desires to have vast secrets held away from him. Scientology has slashed through many of the complexities which have been erected for men and has bared the core of these

---

2. **studiously:** zealously, wholeheartedly, deliberately.

problems. Scientology for the first time in man's history can predictably raise intelligence, increase ability, bring about a return of the ability to play a game, and permits man to escape from the dwindling spiral of his own disabilities. Therefore work itself can become again a pleasant and happy thing.

There is one thing which has been learned in Scientology which is very important to the state of mind of the workman. One very often feels in his society that he is working for the immediate paycheck and that he does not gain for the whole society anything of any importance. He does not know several things. One of these is how few good workmen are. On the level of executives, it is interesting to note how precious any large company finds a man really is who can handle and control jobs and men. Such people are rare. All the empty space in the structure of this workaday world is at the top.

And there is another thing which is quite important, and that is the fact that the world today has been led to believe, by mental philosophies calculated to betray it, that when one is dead it is all over and done with and that one has no further responsibility for anything. It is highly doubtful that this is true. One inherits tomorrow what he died out of yesterday.

Another thing we know is that men are not dispensable. It is a mechanism of old philosophies to tell men that if they think they are indispensable they should go down to the graveyard and take a look—those men were indispensable, too. This is the sheerest foolishness. If you really looked carefully in the graveyard, you would find the machinist who set the models going in yesteryear and without whom there would be no industry today. It is doubtful if such a feat is being performed just now. A workman is not just a workman. A laborer is not just a laborer. An office worker is not just an office worker. They are living, breathing, important pillars on which the entire structure of our civilization is erected. They are not cogs in a mighty machine. They are the machine itself.

We have come to a low level of the ability to work. Offices depend very often on no more than one or two men, and the additional staffs seem to add only complexity to the activities of the scene. Countries move forward on the production of just a few factories. It is as though the world were being held together by a handful of desperate men who by working themselves to death may keep the rest of the world going, but again they may not. It is to them that this book is dedicated.

The End

Appendices

Recovery
from Injury

If somebody is injured, you can assist in many ways. Recovery from a burn or bruise or even sprains or breaks is much swifter with Scientology assists.[1]

The most elementary assist is easily done. For ages man has known that "laying on of hands" or Mother's kiss was effective therapy. Even gripping, in pain, an injured member, seems to help. But man neglected the most important part of "laying on of hands." This follows.

Do this exactly and do it with a minimum of talk.

Place your index finger or fingers or palm on the injured member, very lightly, and say to the person, "Put your attention on my hand." Now change the position of your finger or palm and have the person do it again.

It is best to touch the individual on spots which are further from his *head* than the *injury*.

Do not talk excessively. But coax him, as you touch, briefly,

---

1. **assists:** simple, easily done processes that can be applied to anyone to help them recover more rapidly from accidents, mild illness or upsets.

spot after spot, to put his attention on your finger or fingers or palm.

Change the spot every moment or two. Be calm. Be reassuring.

If the person experiences pain or trembling as a result, keep on, for the assist is working.

Continue in this fashion for many minutes or half an hour if necessary, until pain or upset is gone.

During this assist the person has his eyes closed.

It is not power from your finger which is aiding him. It is power he generates by "looking" at your finger down through his body. You are putting him into communication with the injury. His communication with it brings about the recovery.

Ordinarily injuries, sprains, burns, scalds, broken bones, headaches and colds heal slowly because the individual is avoiding this area with his own energy.

An assist is not a substitute for medical attention and does not attempt to cure injuries requiring medical aid. First call a doctor. Then assist the person as you can.

How to
Handle Work

D₀ it now.

One of the best ways to cut your work in half is not to do it twice.

Probably your most fruitful source of dev-t[1] is your own double work.

This is the way you do double work.

You pick up a despatch or a piece of work, look it over and then put it aside to do later, then later you pick it up and read it again and only then do you do it.

This of course doubles your traffic just like that.

One of the reasons I can handle so much traffic is that I don't do it twice. I make it a heavy rule that if I find myself

---

1. **dev-t:** abbreviation for developed traffic; *developed traffic* does not mean usual and necessary traffic [flow of persons or messages along communication lines]. It means unusual and unnecessary traffic, a great many motions necessary where only the one correct one was needed.

---

handling a piece of traffic, I handle it, not put it into a hold or a later category.

If I happen to be prowling through my basket in the message center stack to see what's there, I do what I find there.

If I am given a message or a datum that requires further action from me, I do it right when I receive it.

This is how I buy "loafing time."

Now, I'm not trying to hold me up as a model of virtue, as the man who always does his job. I do many jobs and many hats.[2] I am holding myself up as an ambitious loafer and as a buyer of valuable loafing time.

There's no need to look busy if you are not busy.

There is no need to fondle[3] and caress work because there isn't enough of it.

There's plenty of work to do. The best answer to work of any kind is to do it.

If you do every piece of work that comes your way *when* it comes your way and not after a while, if you always take the initiative and take action, not refer[4] it, you never get any traffic back unless you've got a psycho on the other end.

---

2. **hats:** particular duties in an organization. Developed in 1950 for use in Dianetics organizations as a special technology, the term and idea of a hat comes from conductors or locomotive engineers, etc., each of whom wears a distinctive and different type of headgear.

3. **fondle:** to handle or treat with fondness.

4. **refer:** to send or direct (to someone or something) for aid, information, consideration or decision.

In short, the way to get rid of traffic is to do it, not to refer it; anything referred has to be read by you again, digested again, and handled again; so never refer traffic, just do it so it's done.

You can keep a comm line in endless foment[5] by pretending that the easiest way not to work is to not handle things or to refer things. Everything you don't handle comes back and bites. Everything you refer has to be done when it comes back to you.

So, if you are truly a lover of ease, the sort of person who yawns comfortably and wears holes in his heels resting them on desks, if your true ambition is one long bout of spring fever,[6] then you'll do as I suggest and handle everything that comes your way when it comes and not later, and you'll never refer anything to anybody that you yourself can do promptly.

That people begin to point you out as a model of efficiency, as the thing expected to cop the next world's speed record, that articles begin to appear about the marvels you are creating, is all incidental. You and I know we did it so we could be lazy and not have to work. For it can be truly said that the way to all labor of a long and continuous grind is by putting off the action when the message is received and in referring it all to somebody else. That's the way to slavery, to tired muscles and tattered brains. That's the route to baskets piled high.

So come loaf with me.

Do it when you see it and do it yourself.

---

5. **foment:** a state of excitation.

6. **spring fever:** the laziness and listlessness that many people feel during the first warm, sunny days of spring.

About the Author

L. Ron Hubbard is known as the most celebrated writer of self-betterment books in the world today, and for a very important reason—his writing expresses a firsthand knowledge of life and the nature of man.

As Ron said, "One doesn't learn about life by sitting in an ivory tower, thinking about it. One learns about life by being part of it." And that is how he lived.

Born in Tilden, Nebraska, on 13 March 1911, his life was anything but sheltered. He was brought up in the rough environment of Montana where he learned very quickly that survival depended utterly on personal ability.

In his early teens, Ron traveled extensively. By the age of nineteen he had traveled a quarter of a million miles, including voyages to China, Japan and other points in the Orient and South Pacific, and had become closely acquainted with twenty-one different races in areas all over the world.

After returning to the United States, he attended George Washington University, where he studied engineering, higher mathematics and was even a member of one of the first American classes in nuclear physics ever taught.

Throughout his travels, his formal studies and his own professional activities, Ron never deviated from his primary purpose of providing mankind with a workable technology to improve life. He had realized that there *was* no real technology of the human mind and found that the "technologies" which mental practitioners had evolved on this planet were in fact barbarisms. He was determined to find a solution to this through his studies of mankind and life.

The tremendous results of his research first came into broad public view in May 1950 with the publication of *Dianetics: The Modern Science of Mental Health*. This book immediately became a best seller. It was the first book of its kind—a practical textbook on the mind that any layman could read, apply and directly use to experience increased awareness, relief from unwanted physical conditions and a new life.

Ron's discoveries led him further and further into the realm of the human spirit. Breakthrough after breakthrough followed, each pushing aside previously insurmountable barriers, enabling man to achieve states of existence never before envisioned. These advances were codified and became the principal tenets of Scientology—a workable way to improve life in this troubled world.

Problems of Work was written by Ron to help solve the difficulties people encounter handling one of the most important parts of their lives—working. In this book he channeled the far-reaching capability of Scientology technology to the working world. Using just some of the materials in this book, people have learned to overcome job difficulties and problems related to their work that had earlier seemed inescapable and overwhelming.

Ron dedicated his life to helping others and to developing techniques that would ensure the route to a higher level of understanding could be traveled by anyone.

His works—including an astounding number of books, taped lectures, instructional films, writings, demonstrations and briefings—are studied and applied in hundreds of Dianetics and Scientology organizations all over the world. Additionally, millions of individuals spanning every continent apply his technology daily in their own homes, schools and workplaces to improve their lives and those of friends, family and co-workers.

With his research fully completed and codified, L. Ron Hubbard departed his body on 24 January 1986.

The spiritual technology he has given mankind makes it possible for us to achieve Ron's dream, "A civilization without insanity, without criminals and without war, where the able can prosper and honest beings can have rights, and where man is free to rise to greater heights."

His works make this dream attainable. Applying his technology is all that is needed to achieve it.

Glossary

Aberration: a departure from rational thought or behavior. From the Latin, *aberrare*, "to wander from"; Latin, *ab*, "away," *errare*, "to wander." It means basically to err, to make mistakes, or more specifically to have fixed ideas which are not true. The word is also used in its scientific sense. It means departure from a straight line. If a line should go from A to B and it is "aberrated," it would go from A to some other point, to some other point, to some other point, to some other point, to some other point and finally arrive at B. Taken in its scientific sense, it would also mean the lack of straightness or to see crookedly as, for example, a man sees a horse but thinks he sees an elephant. Aberrated conduct would be wrong conduct, or conduct not supported by reason. Aberration is opposed to sanity which would be its opposite.

adept: highly skilled; expert.

advisedly: with due consideration; deliberately.

aligned: placed in line, brought into line.

analytical mind: the conscious, aware mind which thinks, observes data, remembers it, and resolves problems. It would be essentially the conscious mind as opposed to the unconscious mind. In Dianetics and Scientology, the analytical mind is the one which is alert and aware and the reactive mind simply reacts without analysis.

Anglo-American: belonging to, relating to or involving England and America, especially the United States, or the people of the two countries.

antipathy: a strong or deep-rooted dislike.

arduous: needing much effort; laborious.

aspirant: a person who has ambition toward something.

assists: simple, easily done processes that can be applied to anyone to help them recover more rapidly from accidents, mild illness or upsets.

auditing: the application of Scientology processes and procedures to someone by a trained auditor.

auditor: a person trained and qualified in applying Scientology and/or Dianetic processes and procedures to individuals for their betterment; called an auditor because *auditor* means "one who listens."

axioms: statements of natural laws on the order of those of the physical sciences.

balk: to obstruct or hinder.

beingness: the assumption or choosing of a category of identity. Beingness is assumed by oneself or given to oneself or is attained. Examples of beingness would be one's own name, one's profession, one's physical characteristics, one's role in a game—each and all of these things could be called one's beingness.

breaks: chance pieces of luck, often specifically of good luck.

cabal: a secret plot.

capital: wealth (money or property) owned or used in business by a person, corporation, etc.

chastise: to scold or condemn sharply.

circuit: a part of an individual's mind that behaves as though it were someone or something separate from him and either dictates or takes over his actions.

close: thorough; careful.

communication lines: routes along which communication travels from one person to another; any sequences through which a message of any character may go.

concern: a business establishment.

convulsion: any violent disturbance, as a social upheaval or an earthquake.

countenance: support, approve or tolerate.

cynical: believing that people are motivated in all their actions only by selfishness; denying the sincerity of people's motives and actions or the value of living.

depression: a period during which business, employment and stock market values decline severely and remain at a very low level of activity.

despondent: feeling or showing profound hopelessness or discouragement.

despotic: having unrestricted power.

dev-t: abbreviation for developed traffic; *developed traffic* does not mean usual and necessary traffic [flow of persons or messages along communication lines]. It means unusual and unnecessary traffic, a great many motions necessary where only the one correct one was needed.

Dianetics: man's most advanced school of the mind. *Dianetics* means "through the soul" (from Greek *dia*, through, and *nous*, soul). *Dianetics* is further defined as "what the soul is doing to the body." It is a way of handling the energy of which life is made in such a way as to bring about a greater efficiency in the organism and in the spiritual life of the individual.

Dickens, Charles: (1812–70) English novelist of the late nineteenth century whose books are noted for picturesque and extravagant characters in the lower economic strata of England at that time.

disabused: disillusioned; having had one's ideals taken away; made disappointed.

discount: to disbelieve or disregard entirely; set aside as inaccurate or irrelevant.

dispensaries: rooms or places, as in schools, camps or factories, where medicines and first-aid treatment are available.

doctrine: something taught; teachings.

dowager: a widow with a title or property derived from her dead husband.

down scale: into the lower-level emotions, such as apathy, anger, etc.

dynasties: successions of rulers who are members of the same family.

efficiency: accomplishment of or ability to accomplish a job with a minimum expenditure of time and effort.

emotional tone: the general condition of an individual. *See also* **Tone Scale** in this glossary.

fallacy: a deceptive, misleading or false notion, belief, etc.

flukes: accidental strokes of good luck.

foment: a state of excitation.

fondle: to handle or treat with fondness.

front: an appearance, usually pretended or assumed, of social standing, wealth, etc.

gargantuan: gigantic, enormous, colossal.

hats: particular duties in an organization. Developed in 1950 for use in Dianetics organizations as a special technology, the term and idea of a hat comes from conductors or locomotive engineers, etc., each of whom wears a distinctive and different type of headgear.

have it down pat: to know or have memorized thoroughly.

havingness: the concept of being able to reach. By havingness we mean owning, possessing, being capable of commanding, taking charge of objects, energies and spaces.

Hitler, Adolf: (1889–1945) dictator of Germany from 1933 to 1945. In rising to power in Germany, he fortified his position through murder of real or imagined opponents and maintained police-state control over the population. He lead Germany into World War II resulting in its nearly total destruction.

Homer: semilegendary Greek poet of circa eighth century B.C.

ideology: the principal ideas or beliefs that characterize a particular class, group or movement.

incident: liable to happen, accompanying something.

industry: getting things done actively and purposefully; application of energy or purpose to work.

inspiration: the fact or condition of being animated or influenced by a feeling, idea, impulse, etc.

intention: something that one wishes to do. It is an impulse toward something, an idea that one is going to accomplish something. It is intentional, which means one *means* to do it.

invalidate: refute or degrade or discredit or deny something someone else considers to be fact.

involved: complicated.

lights, according to (one's own): following one's own ideas, intelligence and conscience in the best way that one knows.

livingness: the activity of going along a certain course, impelled (driven) by a purpose and with some place to arrive.

Logics: methods of thinking.

lot: one's position in life; fortune.

Lotus Isles: also Lotus Lands. In the *Odyssey* by Homer, the hero, Ulysses, and his crew were driven to the land of the Lotus Eaters. These were people who ate the fruit of a plant that caused a man to lose all memory of his homeland and family. Ulysses had to force his crew back to their ship to be able to leave at all.

Marx, Karl: (1818–83) German political philosopher. Regarded by some as the founder of modern socialism.

maxim: a concisely expressed principle or rule of conduct, or a statement of a general truth.

misemotion: anything that is unpleasant emotion such as antagonism, anger, fear, grief, apathy or a death feeling.

M.I.T. Massachusetts Institute of Technology, a university in Massachusetts specializing in the teaching of science and technology.

Napoleon Bonaparte: (1769–1821) French military leader. He rose to power in France by military force, declared himself emperor and conducted campaigns of conquest across Europe until his final defeat by armies allied against him in 1815.

neurotic: behavior characterizing one who is insane or disturbed on some subject (as opposed to a psychotic person, who is just insane in general).

notoriously: talked or known about widely, but in an unfavorable way.

obsessed: haunted or troubled in the mind; preoccupied greatly.

obsessive: of or having to do with a persistent drive or urge a person cannot control.

occasion: to cause or bring about.

ologies: branches of learning; science: a humorous usage.

overfixed: too set or intent upon something; steadily directed to an excessive degree.

overt acts: intentionally committed harmful acts committed in an effort to resolve a problem.

palatable: acceptable to the mind.

par: average or normal state, condition, degree, etc.

particular: a single thing among a number considered by itself; an individual thing or article.

percentile: percentage.

perpetrated: done or performed (something evil, criminal or offensive); been guilty of.

pined: felt an intense longing.

plane: a level of development, achievement, existence, etc.

preclear: a person who, through Scientology processing, is finding out more about himself and life.

present time: the time which is now and which becomes the past almost as rapidly as it is observed. It is a term loosely applied to the environment existing in now.

privation: lack of the ordinary necessities or comforts of life.

process: a set of questions asked by an auditor to help a person find out things about himself or life.

processing: the application of Scientology processes and procedures to someone by a trained auditor. *See also* **auditor** in this glossary.

propitiative: acting in a manner calculated to reduce the anger or win the favor of another; trying to make calm or quiet.

purchase: a hold or position of advantage for accomplishing something.

qualms: sudden feelings of uneasiness or doubt; misgivings.

rabble-rousers: persons who try to arouse people to violent action by appeals to emotions, prejudices, etc.

ramifications: derived effects, consequences or results.

randomness: condition of being without definite aim, purpose or method, or adherence to a prior arrangement; existing in a haphazard way.

reactive mind: the portion of the mind which works on a stimulus-response basis (given a certain stimulus it will automatically give a certain response) which is not under a person's volitional control and which exerts force and power over a person's awareness, purposes, thoughts, body and actions.

refer: to send or direct (to someone or something) for aid, information, consideration or decision.

regime: a form or manner of government or rule.

remunerative: rewarding; profitable; well-paid.

restimulated: having a past memory reactivated due to similar circumstances in the present approximating circumstances of the past.

scant: inadequate in size or amount; not enough; meager.

Scientology: Scientology applied religious philosophy. It is the study and handling of the spirit in relationship to itself, universes and other life. *Scientology* means *scio*, "knowingness in the fullest sense of the word," and *logos*, "study." In itself the word means literally *knowing how to know*. Scientology is a "route," a way, rather than a dissertation or an assertive body of knowledge. Through its drills and studies one may find the truth for himself. The technology is therefore not expounded as something to believe, but something to *do*.

shortsighted: (1) lacking in foresight. (2) able to see clearly only what is close.

slander: the utterance in the presence of another person of a false statement or statements, damaging to a third person's character or reputation.

spring fever: the laziness and listlessness that many people feel during the first warm, sunny days of spring.

studiously: zealously, wholeheartedly, deliberately.

stunted: stopped or slowed down, hindered.

subapathy: a level below apathy, so low as to constitute a no-affinity, no-emotion, no-problem, no-consequence state of mind on things which are actually tremendously important.

terminal: anything used in a communication system; anything that can receive, relay or send a communication; a man would be a terminal, but a post (position, job or duty to which a person is assigned) would also be a terminal.

tinsel: showy; gaudy.

Tone Scale: the scale of emotional states which range from death at the bottom, up through apathy, grief, fear, covert hostility, anger, antagonism, boredom, conservatism, cheerfulness to enthusiasm at the top. [Actually higher and lower tone levels exist than those named.]

training pattern: a stimulus-response mechanism set up by the analytical mind to carry out activity of either a routine or an emergency nature.

true-blue: unwaveringly faithful or loyal.

unpositive: not precise; not specific.

Vedic hymns: the sacred books of the Hindus. These were religious hymns comprising some 125,000–150,000 volumes.

verve: vigor and energy, as in movement, etc.

volitional: of or having to do with a person's own power of choice.

wherewithal: the things (especially money) needed for a purpose.

workaday: of or having to do with working days; characteristic of a work day or its occupations.

young'un: slang for "young one" or child.

Index

Books and Tapes
by L. Ron Hubbard

Basic Scientology Books

You've read *The Problems of Work*. Now get the rest of the Basic Scientology Books Package. The Basic Scientology Books Package contains the knowledge you need to be able to improve conditions in life. These books are available individually or as a set, complete with an attractive slipcase.

A New Slant on Life • Have you ever asked yourself who am I? What am I? This book of articles by L. Ron Hubbard answers these all too common questions. This is knowledge one can use every day—for a new, more confident and happier slant on life!

Scientology: The Fundamentals of Thought • Improve life *and* make a better world with this easy-to-read book that lays out the fundamental truths about life and thought. No such knowledge has ever before existed, and no such results have ever before been attainable as those which can be reached by the use of this knowledge. Equipped with this book alone, one could perform seeming miracles in changing the states of health, ability and intelligence of people. This *is* how life works. This *is* how you change men, women and children for the better, and attain greater personal freedom.

Scientology 0-8: The Book of Basics • What is life? Did you know an individual can create space, energy and time? Here are the basics of life itself, and the secrets of becoming cause over any area of your life. Discover how you can use the data in this book to achieve your goals.

Basic Dictionary of Dianetics and Scientology • Compiled from the works of L. Ron Hubbard, this convenient dictionary contains the terms and expressions needed by anyone learning Dianetics and Scientology technology. And a *special bonus*—an easy-to-read Scientology organizing board chart that shows you who to contact for services and information at your nearest Scientology organization.

Basic Dianetics Books

The Basic Dianetics Books Package is your complete guide to the inner workings of the mind. You can get all of these books individually or in a set, complete with an attractive slipcase.

Dianetics: The Modern Science of Mental Health • Acclaimed as the most effective self-help book ever published. Dianetics technology has helped millions reach new heights of freedom and ability. Millions of copies are sold every year! Discover the source of mental barriers that prevent you from achieving your goals—and how to handle them!

The Dynamics of Life • Break through the barriers to your happiness. This is the first book Ron wrote detailing the startling principles behind Dianetics—facts so powerful they can change forever the way you look at yourself and your potentials. Discover how you can use the powerful basic principles in this book to blast through the barriers of your mind and gain full control over your success, future and happiness.

Self Analysis • The complete do-it-yourself handbook for anyone who wants to improve their abilities and success potential. Use the simple, easy-to-learn techniques in *Self Analysis* to build self-confidence and reduce stress.

Dianetics: The Evolution of a Science • It is estimated that we use less than ten percent of our mind's potential. What stops us from developing and using the full potential of our minds? *Dianetics: The Evolution of a Science* is L. Ron Hubbard's incredible story of how he discovered the reactive mind and how he developed the keys to unlock its secrets. Get this firsthand account of what the mind really is, and how you can release its hidden potential.

Advanced Scientology Books Package

All the following books contain the knowledge of a spiritual being's relationship to this universe and how his abilities to operate successfully in it can be restored. You can get all of these books individually or in a set, complete with an attractive slipcase.

Scientology 8-80 • What are the laws of life? We are all familiar with physical laws such as the law of gravity, but what laws govern life and thought? L. Ron Hubbard answers the riddles of life and its goals in the physical universe.

Scientology 8-8008 • Get the basic truths about your nature as a spiritual being and your relationship to the physical universe around you. Here, L. Ron Hubbard describes procedures designed to increase your abilities to heights previously only dreamed of.

Scientology: A History of Man • A fascinating look at the evolutionary background and history of the human race. This was Ron's first book on the vast time track of man. As Ron said, "This is a cold-blooded and factual account of your last sixty trillion years."

The Creation of Human Ability • This book contains processes designed to restore the power of a thetan over his own postulates, to understand the nature of his beingness, to free his self-determinism and much, much more.

Dianetics Graduate Books

These books by L. Ron Hubbard give you detailed knowledge of how the mind works—data you can use to help yourself and others break out of the traps of life. While you can get these books individually, the Dianetics Graduate Books Package can also be purchased as a set, complete with an attractive slipcase.

Science of Survival • If you ever wondered how people act the way they do, you'll find this book a wealth of information. It's vital to anyone who wants to understand others and improve personal relationships. *Science of Survival* is built around a remarkable chart—The Hubbard Chart of Human Evaluation. With it you can understand and predict other people's behavior and reactions and greatly increase your control over your own life. This is a valuable handbook that can make a difference between success and failure on the job and in life.

Dianetics 55! • Your success in life depends on your ability to communicate. Do you know a formula exists for communication? Learn the rules of better communication that can help you live a more fulfilling life. Here, L. Ron Hubbard deals with the fundamental principles of communication and how you can master these to achieve your goals.

Advanced Procedure and Axioms • For the *first* time the basics of thought and the physical universe have been codified into a set of fundamental laws, signaling an entirely new way to view and approach the subjects of man, the physical universe and even life itself.

Handbook for Preclears • Written as an advanced personal workbook, *Handbook for Preclears* contains easily done processes to help you overcome the effect of times you were not in control of your life, times that your emotions were a barrier to your success and much more. Completing all the fifteen auditing steps contained in this book sets you up for really being in *control* of your environment and life.

Child Dianetics • Here is a revolutionary new approach to rearing children with Dianetics auditing techniques. Find out how you can help your child achieve greater confidence, more self-reliance, improved learning rate and a happier, more loving relationship with you.

Notes on the Lectures of L. Ron Hubbard • Compiled from his fascinating lectures given shortly after the publication of *Dianetics*, this book contains some of the first material Ron ever released on the ARC Triangle and the Tone Scale, and how these discoveries relate to auditing.

Other Scientology Books

Purification: An Illustrated Answer to Drugs • Do toxins and drugs hold down your ability to think clearly? What is the Purification Program and how does it work? How can harmful chemical substances be gotten out of the body? Our society is ridden by abuse of drugs, alcohol and medicine that reduce one's ability to think clearly. Find out what can be done in this introduction to the Purification Program.

All About Radiation • Can the effects of radiation exposure be avoided or reduced? What exactly would happen in the event of an atomic explosion? Get the answers to these and many other questions in this illuminating book. *All About Radiation* describes observations and discoveries concerning the physical and mental effects of radiation and the possibilities for handling them. Get the real facts on the subject of radiation and its effects.

Have You Lived Before This Life? • This is the book that sparked a flood of interest in the ancient puzzle: Does man live only one life? The answer lay in mystery, buried until L. Ron Hubbard's researches unearthed the truth. Actual case histories of people recalling past lives in auditing tell the tale.

Dianetics and Scientology Technical Dictionary • This dictionary is your indispensable guide to the words and ideas of Scientology and Dianetics technologies—technologies which can help you increase your know-how and effectiveness in life. Over three thousand words are defined—including a new understanding of vital words like *life, love* and *happiness* as well as Scientology terms.

Modern Management Technology Defined: Hubbard Dictionary of Administration and Management • Here's a real breakthrough in the subject of administration and management! Eighty-six hundred words are defined for greater understanding of any business situation. Clear, precise Scientology definitions describe many previously baffling phenomena and bring truth, sanity and understanding to the often murky field of business management.

How to Live Though an Executive • What are the factors in business and commerce which, if lacking, can keep a person overworked and worried, keep labor and management at each other's throats, and make an unsafe working atmosphere? L. Ron Hubbard reveals principles based on years of research into many different types of organizations.

Introduction to Scientology Ethics • A complete knowledge of ethics is vital to anyone's success in life. Without knowing and applying the information in this book, success is only a matter of luck or chance. That is not much to look forward to. This book contains the answers to questions like, "How do I know when a decision is right or wrong?" "How can I predictably improve things around me?" The powerful ethics technology of L. Ron Hubbard is your way to ever-increasing survival.

Organization Executive Course • The *Organization Executive Course* volumes contain organizational technology never before known to man. This is not just how a Scientology organization works; this is how the operation of *any* organization, *any* activity, can be improved. A person knowing the data in these volumes fully, and applying it, could completely reverse any downtrend in a company — or even a country!

Management Series Volume 1 and 2 • These books contain technology that anyone who works with management in any way must know completely to be a true success. Contained in these books are such subjects as data evaluation, the technology of how to organize any area for maximum production and expansion, how to handle personnel, the actual technology of public relations and much more.

Background and Ceremonies of the Church of Scientology • Discover the beautiful and inspiring ceremonies of the Church of Scientology, and its fascinating religious and historical background. This book contains the illuminating Creed of the Church, church services, sermons and ceremonies, many as originally given in person by L. Ron Hubbard, Founder of Scientology.

What is Scientology? • Scientology applied religious philosophy has attracted great interest and attention since its beginning. What is Scientology philosophy? What can it accomplish—and why are so many people from all walks of life proclaiming its effectiveness? Find the answers to these questions and many others in *What is Scientology?*

Introductory and Demonstration Processes and Assists • How can you help someone increase his enthusiasm for living? How can you improve someone's self-confidence on the job? Here are basic Scientology processes you can use to help others deal with life and living.

Volunteer Minister's Handbook • This is a big, practical how-to-do-it book to give a person the basic knowledge on how to help self and others through the rough spots in life. It consists of twenty-one sections—each one covering important situations in life, such as drug and alcohol problems, study difficulties, broken marriages, accidents and illnesses, a failing business, difficult children, and much more. This is the basic tool you need to help someone out of troubles, and bring about a happier life.

The Personal Achievement Series

There are nearly three thousand recorded lectures by L. Ron Hubbard on the subjects of Dianetics and Scientology. What follows is a sampling of these lectures, each known and loved the world over. All of these are presented in Clearsound state-of-the-art sound-recording technology, notable for its clarity and brilliance of reproduction.

Get all the Personal Achievement Series cassettes by L. Ron Hubbard listed below and ask your nearest Scientology church or organization or the publisher about future releases.

The Story of Dianetics and Scientology • In this lecture, L. Ron Hubbard shares with you his earliest insights into human nature and gives a compelling and often humorous account of his experiences. Spend an unforgettable time with Ron as he talks about the start of Dianetics and Scientology!

The Road to Truth • The road to truth has eluded man since the beginning of time. In this classic lecture, L. Ron Hubbard explains what this road actually is and why it is the only road one MUST travel all the way once begun. This lecture reveals the only road to higher levels of living.

Scientology and Effective Knowledge • Voyage to new horizons of awareness! *Scientology and Effective Knowledge* by L. Ron Hubbard can help you understand more about yourself and others. A fascinating tale of the beginnings of Dianetics and Scientology.

The Deterioration of Liberty • What do governments fear so much in a population that they amass weapons to defend themselves from people? Find out from Ron in this classic lecture.

Power of Choice and Self-Determinism • Man's ability to determine the course of his life depends on his ability to exercise his power of choice. Find out how you can increase your power of choice and self-determinism in life from Ron in this lecture.

Scientology and Ability • Ron points out that this universe is here because we perceive it and agree to it. Applying Scientology principles to life can bring new adventure to life and put you on the road to discovering better beingness.

The Hope of Man • Various men in history brought forth the idea that there was hope of improvement. But L. Ron Hubbard's discoveries in Dianetics and Scientology have made that hope a reality. Find out by listening to this lecture how Scientology has become man's one, true hope for his final freedom.

The Dynamics • In this lecture Ron gives incredible data on the dynamics: how man creates on them, what happens when a person gets stuck in just one, how wars relate to the third dynamic and much more.

Money • Ron talks in this classic lecture about that subject which makes or breaks men with the greatest of ease—money. Find out what money really is and gain greater control over your own finances.

Formulas for Success—*The Five Conditions* • How does one achieve real success? It sometimes appears that luck is the primary factor, but the truth of the matter is that natural laws exist which govern the conditions of life. These laws have been discovered by Ron, and in this lecture he gives you the exact steps to take in order to improve conditions in any aspect of your life.

Health and Certainty • You need certainty of yourself in order to achieve the success you want in life. In *Health and Certainty*, L. Ron Hubbard tells how you can achieve certainty and really be free to think for yourself. Get this tape now and start achieving your full potential!

Man: Good or Evil? • In this lecture, L. Ron Hubbard explores the greatest mystery that has confronted modern science and philosophy—the true nature of man's livingness and beingness. Is man simply a sort of wind-up doll or clock—or worse, an evil beast with no control of his cravings? Or is he capable of reaching higher levels of ability, awareness and happiness? Get this tape and find out the *real* answers.

More advanced books and lectures are available. Contact your nearest organization or write directly to the publisher for a full catalog.

"The success level of a person *is* his communication level."

—*L. Ron Hubbard*

Your success on the job, in handling a home, in creating relationships based on *honesty* and *trust* depends on *your ability to communicate.*

The *Success Through Communication Course* by L. Ron Hubbard is a vital and *practical* course to help you improve communication and be more effective in life. Discover the eighteen exact, simple and powerful techniques that will show you how to:

- Get your point across and really be understood!
- Begin a conversation with anyone—even with a silent person!
- Listen effectively!
- Handle any upset in communication!
- End any conversation when you want to

  —*and much more!*

Learn these effective communication techniques on weekdays, evenings or weekends.

Do the *Success Through Communication Course* by L. Ron Hubbard

Start today!

Contact the Public Registrar at your nearest Church of Scientology.

(A complete list of Scientology Churches or Organizations and their addresses is provided at the back of this book.)

Improve Your Life with Scientology Extension Courses

Scientology books by L. Ron Hubbard give you the knowledge to achieve a happier, more successful life. Now learn to take and *use* that knowledge to gain greater control of *your* life. Enroll on a Scientology Extension Course.

Each extension course package includes a lesson book with easy-to-understand instructions and all the lessons you will need to complete it. Each course can be done in the comfort of your own home or right in your local Scientology organization. Your Extension Course Supervisor will review each lesson as you complete it (or mail it in if you do the course at home) and get the results right back to you. When you complete the course you get a beautiful certificate, suitable for framing.

The Problems of Work Extension Course

Trying to handle a job and keep it can get to be a deadlier struggle with each working day. What are the secrets to increasing your enjoyment of work? How can you gain the personal satisfaction of doing your work well? Find the answers and apply them easily. Do *The Problems of Work Extension Course!*

A New Slant on Life
Extension Course

Life does not have to remain the same. You *can* reach higher levels of knowledge, ability and freedom. Discover the two rules for happy living, the secret of success, how to avoid being a "cog in a machine," how to reach your goals and more. Do the *New Slant on Life Extension Course* and gain a refreshing new outlook on life!

The Fundamentals of Thought
Extension Course

Here is *practical, workable* knowledge that can improve your life in today's troubled world. This extension course will help you gain a far greater understanding of life than you ever thought possible. Order your copy of *The Fundamentals of Thought Extension Course* today!

Enroll on a
Scientology Home Study
Extension Course Today!

For information and enrollment and prices for these extension courses and the books they accompany, contact the Public Registrar at your nearest Church of Scientology. (A complete list of Scientology Churches and Organizations is provided at the back of this book.)

For more information about Scientology or to order books and cassettes

Call: **1-800-367-8788**
in the U.S. and Canada

Is there such a thing as a hotline that doesn't believe in giving advice? What about a hotline for able individuals to help them solve their *own* problems?

"If we take a man and keep giving him advice," L. Ron Hubbard has said, "we don't necessarily wind up with a resolution of his problems. But if, on the other hand, we put him in a position where he had higher intelligence, where his reaction time was better, where he could confront life better, where he could identify the factors in his life more easily, then he's in a position where he can solve his own problems."

Call the unique new hotline and referral service with operators trained in Scientology technology. Callers find someone they can trust to talk to about a problem, and they are referred to their nearest Scientology church or organization for more information if they are interested.

You can also order books and cassettes by L. Ron Hubbard by calling this number.

Call this toll-free number
7 days a week
from 9 A.M. to 11 P.M. Pacific Standard Time.

Get Your Free Catalog
of Knowledge on
How to Improve Life

L. Ron Hubbard's books and tapes increase your ability to understand yourself and others. His works give you the practical know-how you need to improve your life and the lives of your family and friends.

Many more materials by L. Ron Hubbard are available than have been covered in the pages of this book. A free catalog of these materials is available on request.

Write for your free catalog today!

Bridge Publications, Inc.
4751 Fountain Avenue
Los Angeles, California 90029

NEW ERA Publications International, ApS
Store Kongensgade 55
1264 Copenhagen K, Denmark

"I am always happy to hear from my readers."

L. Ron Hubbard

These were the words of L. Ron Hubbard, who was always very interested in hearing from his friends, readers and followers. He made a point of staying in communication with everyone he came in contact with over his fifty-year career as a professional writer, and he had thousands of fans and friends that he corresponded with all over the world.

The publishers of L. Ron Hubbard's literary works wish to continue this tradition and would welcome letters and comments from you, his readers, both old and new.

Any message addressed to the Author's Affairs Director at Bridge Publications will be given prompt and full attention.

Bridge Publications, Inc.
4751 Fountain Avenue
Los Angeles, California 90029
U.S.A.

Church and Organization Address List

Albuquerque
Church of Scientology
8106 Menaul Blvd. NE
Albuquerque, New Mexico 87110

Ann Arbor
Church of Scientology
301 North Ingalls Street
Ann Arbor, Michigan 48104

Atlanta
Church of Scientology
2632 Piedmonte Rd., NE
Atlanta, Georgia 30324

Austin
Church of Scientology
2200 Guadalupe
Austin, Texas 78705

Boston
Church of Scientology
448 Beacon Street
Boston, Massachusetts 02115

Buffalo
Church of Scientology
47 West Huron Street
Buffalo, New York 14202

Chicago
Church of Scientology
3011 North Lincoln Avenue
Chicago, Illinois 60657

Cincinnati
Church of Scientology
215 West 4th Street, 5th Floor
Cincinnati, Ohio 45202

Clearwater
Church of Scientology
Flag® Service Organization
210 South Fort Harrison Avenue
Clearwater, Florida 34616

Columbus
Church of Scientology
167 East State Street
Columbus, Ohio 43215

Dallas
Church of Scientology
Celebrity Centre® Dallas
8501 Manderville Lane
Dallas, Texas 75231

Denver
Church of Scientology
375 South Navajo Street
Denver, Colorado 80223

Detroit
Church of Scientology
321 Williams Street
Royal Oak, Michigan 48067

Honolulu
Church of Scientology
1 N. King St., Lower Level
Honolulu, Hawaii 96817

Kansas City
Church of Scientology
3619 Broadway
Kansas City, Missouri 64111

Las Vegas
Church of Scientology
846 East Sahara Avenue
Las Vegas, Nevada 89104

Church of Scientology
Celebrity Centre Las Vegas
1100 South 10th Street
Las Vegas, Nevada 89104

Long Island
Church of Scientology
330 Fulton Avenue
Hempstead, New York 11550

Los Angeles and vicinity
Church of Scientology
4810 Sunset Boulevard
Los Angeles, California 90027

Church of Scientology
1451 Irvine Boulevard
Tustin, California 92680

Church of Scientology
263 East Colorado Boulevard
Pasadena, California 91101

Church of Scientology
10335 Magnolia Boulevard
North Hollywood, California 91601

Church of Scientology
American Saint Hill Organization
1413 North Berendo Street
Los Angeles, California 90027

Church of Scientology
American Saint Hill Foundation
1413 North Berendo Street
Los Angeles, California 90027

Church of Scientology
Advanced Organization of
  Los Angeles
1306 North Berendo Street
Los Angeles, California 90027

Church of Scientology
Celebrity Centre International
5930 Franklin Avenue
Hollywood, California 90028

Miami
Church of Scientology
120 Giralda Avenue
Coral Gables, Florida 33134

Minneapolis
Church of Scientology
3019 Minnehaha Avenue
Minneapolis, Minnesota 55406

New Haven
Church of Scientology
909 Whalley Avenue
New Haven, Connecticut 06515

New York City
Church of Scientology
227 West 46th Street
New York City, New York 10036

Church of Scientology
Celebrity Centre New York
65 East 82nd Street
New York City, New York 10028

Orlando
Church of Scientology
710-A East Colonial Drive
Orlando, Florida 32803

Philadelphia
Church of Scientology
1315 Race Street
Philadelphia, Pennsylvania 19107

Phoenix
Church of Scientology
4450 North Central Avenue, Suite 102
Phoenix, Arizona 85012

Portland
Church of Scientology
323 SW Washington
Portland, Oregon 97204

Church of Scientology
Celebrity Centre Portland
709 Southwest Salmon Street
Portland, Oregon 97205

Sacramento
Church of Scientology
825 15th Street
Sacramento, California 95814

San Diego
Church of Scientology
701 "C" Street
San Diego, California 92101

San Francisco
Church of Scientology
83 McAllister Street
San Francisco, California 94102

San Jose
Church of Scientology
80 E. Rosemary
San Jose, California 95112

Santa Barbara
Church of Scientology
524 State Street
Santa Barbara, California 93101

Seattle
Church of Scientology
2004 Westlake Avenue
Seattle, Washington 98121

St. Louis
Church of Scientology
9510 Page Boulevard
St. Louis, Missouri 63132

Tampa
Church of Scientology
4809 North Armenia Avenue
Suite 215
Tampa, Florida 33603

Washington, DC
Founding Church of Scientology
2125 "S" Street NW
Washington, DC 20008

Canada

Edmonton
Church of Scientology
10349 82nd Avenue
Edmonton, Alberta
Canada T6E 1Z9

Kitchener
Church of Scientology
8 Water Street North
Kitchener, Ontario
Canada N2H 5A5

Montréal
Church of Scientology
4489 Papineau Street
Montréal, Québec
Canada H2H 1T7

Ottawa
Church of Scientology
150 Rideau Street, 2nd Floor
Ottawa, Ontario
Canada K1N 5X6

Quebec
Church of Scientology
226 St-Joseph est
Québec, Québec
Canada G1K 3A9

Toronto
Church of Scientology
696 Yonge Street
Toronto, Ontario
Canada M4Y 2A7

Vancouver
Church of Scientology
401 West Hastings Street
Vancouver, British Columbia
Canada V6B 1L5

Winnipeg
Church of Scientology
Suite 125—388 Donald Street
Winnipeg, Manitoba
Canada R3B 2J4

United Kingdom

Birmingham
Church of Scientology
60/62 Constitution Hill
Birmingham
England B5 4TD

Brighton
Church of Scientology
Dukes Arcade, Top Floor
Dukes Street
Brighton, Sussex
England

East Grinstead
Saint Hill Foundation
Saint Hill Manor
East Grinstead, West Sussex
England RH19 4JY

Advanced Organization Saint Hill
Saint Hill Manor
East Grinstead, West Sussex
England RH19 4JY

Edinburgh

Hubbard Academy of Personal
   Independence
20 Southbridge
Edinburgh, Scotland EH1 1LL

London

Church of Scientology
68 Tottenham Court Road
London, England W1P 0BB

Manchester

Church of Scientology
258 Deansgate
Manchester, England M3 4BG

Plymouth

Church of Scientology
41 Ebrington Street
Plymouth, Devon
England PL4 9AA

Sunderland

Church of Scientology
51 Fawcett Street
Sunderland, Tyne and Wear
England SR1 1RS

Austria

Vienna

Church of Scientology
Schottenfeldgasse 13–15
1070 Vienna, Austria

Vienna South

Church of Scientology
Celebrity Centre VNA
Senefelderg. 12
A-1100 Vienna, Austria

Belgium

Brussels

Church of Scientology
45A, rue de l'Ecuyer
1000 Bruxelles, Belgium

Denmark

Aarhus

Church of Scientology
Guldsmedegade 17, 2
8000 Aarhus C, Denmark

Copenhagen

Church of Scientology
Store Kongensgade 55
1264 Copenhagen K, Denmark

Copenhagen (cont.)

Church of Scientology
Vesterbrogade 66
1620 Copenhagen V, Denmark

Church of Scientology
Advanced Organization Saint Hill
   for Europe and Africa
Jernbanegade 6
1608 Copenhagen V, Denmark

France

Angers

Church of Scientology
10–12, rue Max Richard
49000 Angers, France

Clermont-Ferrand

Church of Scientology
2 Pte rue Giscard de la Tour Fondue
63000 Clermont-Ferrand, France

Lyon

Church of Scientology
3, place des Capucins
69001 Lyon, France

Paris

Church of Scientology
65, rue de Dunkerque
75009 Paris, France

Church of Scientology
Celebrity Centre Paris
69, rue Legendre
75017 Paris, France

St. Etienne

Church of Scientology
24, rue Marengo
42000 St. Etienne, France

Germany

Berlin
Church of Scientology e.V.
Sponholzstrasse 51/52
1000 Berlin 41, Germany

Düsseldorf
Church of Scientology
Friedrichstrasse 28
4000 Düsseldorf, West Germany

Church of Scientology
Celebrity Centre Düsseldorf
Grupellostr. 28
4000 Düsseldorf, West Germany

Frankfurt
Church of Scientology
Darmstadter Landstrasse 119–125
6000 Frankfurt/Main, West Germany

Hamburg
Church of Scientology e.V.
Steindamm 63
2000 Hamburg 1, West Germany

Church of Scientology
Celebrity Centre Hamburg
Mönckebergstrasse 5/IV
2000 Hamburg 1
West Germany

Hannover
Church of Scientology
Bodekerstrasse 96
3000 Hannover 1, West Germany

Munich
Church of Scientology e.V.
Beichstrasse 12
D-8000 München 40, West Germany

Greece

Athens
Applied Philosophy Center of Greece
(K.E.F.E.)
Ippokratous 175B
114 72 Athens, Greece

Israel

Tel Aviv
Scientology and Dianetics College
7 Salomon Street
Tel Aviv 66023, Israel

Italy

Brescia
Church of Scientology
Dei Tre Laghi
Via Fratelli Bronzetti N. 20
25125 Brescia, Italy

Milano
Church of Scientology
Via Abetone, 10
20137 Milano, Italy

Monza
Church of Scientology
Via Cavour, 5
20052 Monza, Italy

Novara
Church of Scientology
Corso Cavallotti No. 7
28100 Novara, Italy

Nuoro
Church of Scientology
Corso Garibaldi, 108
08100 Nuoro, Italy

Padua
Church of Scientology
Via Mameli 1/5
35131 Padova, Italy

Pordenone
Church of Scientology
Via Montereale, 10/C
33170 Pordenone, Italy

Rome
Church of Scientology
Via di San Vito, 11
00185 Roma, Italy

Turin
Church of Scientology
Via Guarini, 4
10121 Torino, Italy

Verona
Church of Scientology
Vicolo Chiodo No. 4/A
37121 Verona, Italy

Netherlands

Amsterdam
Church of Scientology
Nieuwe Zijds Voorburgwal 271
1012 RL Amsterdam, Netherlands

Norway

Oslo
Church of Scientology
Storgata 9
0155 Oslo 1, Norway

Portugal

Lisbon
Instituto de Dianética
Rua Actor Taborda 39–4°
1000 Lisboa, Portugal

Spain

Barcelona
Dianética
Calle Pau Claris 85, Principal 1ª
08010 Barcelona, Spain

Madrid
Asociación Civil de Dianética
Montera 20, Piso 1° DCHA
28013 Madrid, Spain

Sweden

Göteborg
Church of Scientology
Odinsgatan 8
411 03 Göteborg, Sweden

Malmö
Church of Scientology
Simrishamnsgatan 10
21423 Malmö, Sweden

Stockholm
Church of Scientology
Kammakargatan 46
S-111 60 Stockholm, Sweden

Switzerland

Basel
Church of Scientology
Herrengrabenweg 56
4054 Basel, Switzerland

Bern
Church of Scientology
Schulhausgasse 12
3113 Rubigen
Bern, Switzerland

Geneva
Church of Scientology
9 Route de Saint-Julien
1227 Carouge
Genève, Switzerland

Lausanne
Church of Scientology
10, rue de la Madeleine
1003 Lausanne, Switzerland

Zürich
Church of Scientology
Badenerstrasse 294
CH-8004 Zürich, Switzerland

Australia

Adelaide
Church of Scientology
24 Waymouth Street
Adelaide, South Australia 5000
Australia

Brisbane
Church of Scientology
2nd Floor, 106 Edward Street
Brisbane, Queensland 4000
Australia

Canberra
Church of Scientology
Suite 16, 108 Bunda Street
Canberra Civic
A.C.T 2601, Australia

Melbourne
Church of Scientology
44 Russell Street
Melbourne, Victoria 3000
Australia

Perth
Church of Scientology
39–41 King Street
Perth, Western Australia 6000
Australia

Sydney
Church of Scientology
201 Castlereagh Street
Sydney, New South Wales 2000
Australia

Church of Scientology
Advanced Organization Saint Hill
 Australia, New Zealand and
 Oceania
19–37 Greek Street
Glebe, New South Wales 2037
Australia

Japan

Tokyo
Scientology Tokyo Org
101 Toyomi Nishi Gotanda Heights
2-13-5 Nishi Gotanda
Shinagawa-Ku
Tokyo, Japan 141

New Zealand

Auckland
Church of Scientology
2nd Floor, 44 Queen Street
Auckland 1, New Zealand

Africa

Bulawayo
Church of Scientology
74 Abercorn Street
Bulawayo, Zimbabwe

Cape Town
Church of Scientology
5 Beckham Street
Gardens
Cape Town 8001, South Africa

Durban
Church of Scientology
57 College Lane
Durban 4001, South Africa

Harare
Church of Scientology
First Floor State Lottery Building
P.O. Box 3524
Corner Speke Avenue and
 Julius Nyerere Way
Harare, Zimbabwe

Johannesburg
Church of Scientology
Security Building, 2nd Floor
95 Commissioner Street
Johannesburg 2001, South Africa

Church of Scientology
101 Huntford Building
40 Hunter Street
Cnr. Hunter & Fortesque Roads
Yeoville 2198
Johannesburg, South Africa

Port Elizabeth
Church of Scientology
2 St. Christopher
27 Westbourne Road
Port Elizabeth 6001, South Africa

Pretoria
Church of Scientology
"Die Meent Arcade,"
 2nd Level, Shop 43b
266 Pretorius Street
Pretoria 0002, South Africa

Latin America

Colombia

Bogotá
Centro Cultural de Dianética
Carrera 19 No. 39–55
Apartado Aereo 92419
Bogotá, D.E. Colombia

Mexico

Estado de México
Instituto Technologico de Dianética,
 A.C.
Londres 38, 5th Floor
Col. Juarez, México D.F.

Guadalajara
Organización Cultural Dianética de
 Guadalajara, A.C.
Av. Lopez Mateos Nte. 329
Sector Hidalgo
Guadalajara, Jalisco, México

Mexico City
Asociación Cultural Dianética, A.C.
Hermes No. 46
Colonia Crédito Constructor
03940 México 19, D.F.

Instituto de Filosofia Aplicada, A.C.
Durango #105
Colonia Roma
06700 México D.F.

Instituto de Filosofia Aplicada, A.C.
Plaza Rio de Janeiro No. 52
Colonia Roma
06700 México D.F.

Organización, Desarrollo y
Dianética, A.C.
Providencia 1000
Colonia Del Valle
C.P. 03100 México D.F.

Centro de Dianética Polanco
Insurgentes Sur 536, 1er piso
Esq. Nogales
Colonia Roma Sur C.P.
06700 México D.F.

Venezuela

Valencia
Asociación Cultural Dianética de
Venezuela, A.C.
Ave. 101 No. 150–23
Urbanizacion La Alegria
Apartado Postal 833
Valencia, Venezuela

To obtain any books or cassettes by L. Ron Hubbard which are not available at your local organization, contact any of the following publishers:

Bridge Publications, Inc.
4751 Fountain Avenue
Los Angeles, California 90029

Continental Publications Liaison Office
696 Yonge Street
Toronto, Ontario
Canada M4Y 2A7

NEW ERA Publications International
ApS
Store Kongensgade 55
1264 Copenhagen K, Denmark

Era Dinámica Editores, S.A. de C.V.
Alabama 105
Colonia Nápoles
C.P. 03810 México, D.F.

NEW ERA Publications, Ltd.
78 Holmethorpe Avenue
Redhill, Surrey RH1 2NL
United Kingdom

N.E. Publications Australia Pty. Ltd.
2 Verona Street
Paddington, New South Wales 2021
Australia

Continental Publications Pty. Ltd.
P.O. Box 27080
Benrose 2011
South Africa

NEW ERA Publications Italia Srl
Via L.G. Columella, 12
20128 Milano, Italy

NEW ERA Publications GmbH
Otto—Hahn—Strasse 25
6072 Dreieich 1, Germany

NEW ERA Publications France
111, Boulevard de Magenta
75010 Paris, France

New Era Publications España, S.A.
C/De la Paz, 4/1° dcha
28012 Madrid, Spain

New Era Japan
5-4-5-803 Nishigotanda
Shinagawa-Ku
Tokyo, Japan 141